THE
PEACE OF MIND
Business

JAY TUERK, YONI ASHUROV, BILL HOFFMANN

with Bill Quain, Ph.D.

The Peace of Mind Business
The Right Time… The Right Place… The Right YOU

By Jay Tuerk, Yoni Ashurov, Bill Hoffmann with Bill Quain, Ph.D.

Cover Design and Layout by Parry Design Studio, Inc.
www.parrydesign.com

Dedications

Jay Tuerk

I dedicate this book to all of my family, friends, and mentors. It is an honor to have you in my life. In particular, many thanks to my children, Sean, Kelly, Nicholas and Matthew, for making me strive to be a better man. I owe a special debt of gratitude to Walter Fiveson and James Mosebrook. Without you, I would not be where I am today. But this book is especially dedicated to you, the MWR Agent, for you are truly the reason I do what I do each and every single day. I ask you to take the pages of this book to heart. Learn what this book has to offer you. And then, take the necessary action to reach the level of success you deserve!

Yoni Ashurov

This book is dedicated to my parents, Alex and Rachel, for always striving for our family's "peace of mind." To my beautiful wife, Evelyn, and our mesmerizing children, Maia and Elia, for continuing to elevate my "peace of mind." And last but not least, for YOU, the brand new MWR Agent, and your triumphant destiny of achieving financial "peace of mind."

Bill Hoffmann

I owe this book to my family—Anne, Ian, Natalie and Will—for their ongoing support over the past 26 years. I also want to thank all of the mentors that were there for me along the way. It is these people that have allowed me to open the door to success and leap forward. And, to each and every one of you brand new MWR Agents, I am pledging to offer my mentorship. I will do whatever I can to help you open your own door to success and achieve that financial peace of mind we all seek.

Acknowledgements

The authors would like to thank the following people for their help and support:

Jeannine Norris for editing, Jack and Elizabeth Parry for cover design and interior layout, Cindy Nevitt for interviews, and a special thank you to Bill Quain, without whom this book would never be possible.

Table of Contents

Disruption:
Remember This Word!

You are about to read a *business book*. This is not a book about just any business. It is a book about *YOUR* business. This will change your life if you just learn a few simple truths about business, people, and how to recognize and seize an opportunity.

And believe us when we tell you this—opportunity is the right word for what you are about to discover. You have an opportunity for one simple reason: you are at the right place, at exactly the right time. You just happen to be right here, when it is all getting started. You are finally just where you need to be.

And, why is this the right time? What makes THIS time, of all times, just the right time for you?

It is the right time because an entire $50 billion dollar industry is about to be completely *disrupted*. That is significant. But, you are also in the right place at the right time because YOU have something that the movers and shakers in this industry are looking for.

Yes, that's right. YOU have just what they want. No, they don't want your money. This isn't an investment opportunity. They want your *action*. They want YOU to help spread the word by sharing this opportunity. You see, because of this incredible disruption, it turns out that you have just what it takes to make some serious money.

"But wait," you are probably saying, "If all I have to do is to share this information with some other people, why do they need me? Wouldn't *anyone* be the right kind of person for this business?"

Well, maybe. But, it isn't just ANYONE who is here, right? YOU are here. YOU are the one reading this book and standing here, right now, ready to take advantage of this disruption. That's why we say *you are at the right place, at the right time.* YOU are.

So, What Is Disruption and Why Will It Help Me Make Money?

Disruption occurs when an industry has done things the same way for a long time, but suddenly, there is a new way of doing things and it takes everyone by surprise. When that happens, most companies can't react quickly enough to changing times. Most companies don't *want* to change anyway. They just aren't equipped to do it. How many executives are going to walk into a meeting and say, "You know how well we have been doing? Well, I think it is all about to change. Maybe we better start from scratch and try it a different way."

Folks, that kind of innovative thinking just doesn't happen, especially when things have been going so well for so long. Everyone is used to doing things a certain way. One company does it that way, and so do their competitors. NO ONE wants to be the one who says, "We better try it another way."

But, you are about to learn about the Warranty Business. The Warranty Business has remained unchanged for decades. A very few warranty companies are working with Big Box Retailers and Auto Dealerships to create over-priced, short-term warranties. It has been the same way since the 70s. (You will read about it in this book.)

What is wrong with that? Why is it about to change? Why *should* it change?

To answer that, let's look at three other industries that underwent huge disruptions.

The Music Industry was one of those old-fashioned businesses: artists recorded records on vinyl, then tapes, and then on plastic CDs. Records were sold in a *record store*, right? (How many of them are left now?) Then, along came Apple, and they invent the iPod, and the digital music industry takes off.

But, it wasn't so easy. Producers and Retailers fought the changes. They insisted that music could only be sold one way. Apple thought differently. Was Apple at the right place at the right time? YES! BILLIONS of dollars went to the people who jumped into iTunes and other digital venues. Today, almost all music is bought online.

Then there's PayPal, which did not exist until 16 years ago. How did people make payments? They used credit cards. If you wanted to buy something, someone swiped your card. You couldn't buy things online very easily. In fact, the online retail market actually struggled until PayPal made it safe and secure.

Did this cause massive upheaval for credit card companies and online and offline retailers? Of course it did! Was there anyone on the *inside* of this business—a person who worked for a major credit card company for example—who was saying, "Let's make some huge changes in the way we do business" BEFORE PayPal came along? Of course not.

But, when PayPal hit the market, it wasn't long before they were getting all the money that credit card companies used to make. And, it wasn't long before EVERYONE was buying through PayPal.

Finally, let's look at the Amazon Kindle. Before it was invented and released, did anyone think, "I will buy books with a few clicks of the mouse, and put them on a book machine without pages to turn?" Absolutely NOT! This thing was a complete disruption. And, Amazon completely changed the book market. Do you still go to bookstores? If you do, it probably isn't to buy books! (By the way, is Amazon in the business of making money on their Kindles? No. They make money when you buy books on Kindle. Why? They can't make much on a single Kindle, *or even thousand or millions* of Kindles. But they make lots of money when you buy book after book after book from Amazon.)

Which Industry Is Next?

You guessed it, the Warranty Industry. Their entire premise—sell something that you don't make much money on (electronics, autos, etc.) and then try to make up the cost of all those expensive stores and employees by selling people warranties that are over-priced and only provide coverage for a limited amount of time. Does that make sense to you?

It didn't make sense to Jay Tuerk. Jay has built one of the largest, independent service contract companies in the United States. He said, "There has to be a better way," and then he did something that almost no one else would think of doing. He CHANGED his business model, and this is what is disrupting the Warranty Industry, right now.

Jay recognized that warranties were too expensive. People don't want to pay out a big chunk of cash when they have already laid out a big chunk of cash for the new computer, television, phone, etc. It just didn't make sense. And, he recognized that the short-term nature of warranties meant that people *lost their coverage just when they were most likely to need it.* That didn't make sense either.

And finally, he had an even bigger, more dangerous (to the established warranty companies and the Big Box Retailers) idea. Jay figured out a way to get you warranties on EVERYTHING you had already bought—up to four years old!

How Does This Affect You?

You may be thinking, "Well, this is all very interesting, but how do I make money? Why do they need me?"

Well, this is where it gets really interesting. You see, Jay knew he needed people just like you to get the word out. He didn't want to spend millions of dollars *in advance* (on advertising) to get sales. Instead, he envisioned he would find some key people who wanted something more out of life. Jay was looking for people who were looking. He brought them a "business in a box." He didn't ask them for a large investment of money. He just asked them to spread the word.

Now THAT is disruptive!

Are You That Person?

Ray Kroc, the founder of McDonald's, had this to add about being at the right place, at the right time: "You have to be at the right place at the right time, *and then do something about it.*"

Well, there is absolutely no doubt about it. You ARE at the right place, and this is the right time. So the only question that remains is: "What are you going to do about it?"

Will you let it pass you by? Will you say, "This probably isn't going to work," or "What are people going to say about me doing this?"

Will you let someone else steal your dream, or keep you from making just a little more each month so that you can pay your bills?

Most importantly, will you let other people take away your Peace of Mind?

Yes, It is THAT Serious!

In this business, you can make a little, or make a lot. You can "dabble" in this business and waste some time, or you can jump into it, and be the right person for this opportunity!

But whatever you do, remember this. We are talking about an opportunity to gain Peace of Mind for once in your life. Worried about money? Stop it—cold!

Do you want to spend more time with loved ones, or travel more? Or maybe you just want to feel like you did something special and that great people noticed what you did and recognized you for it!

Peace of Mind is a gift that you may never have the opportunity to grab again. We are serious about the opportunity, the timing and the disruption. Are you the one who is serious about grabbing the big prize?

Remember, be at the right place, at the right time, and do something about it.

But For Now, Just Read The Book!

Your only job right now is to spend a few hours reading this book. It may not seem like a lot, but you are doing what Ray Kroc said to do. You are at the right place, and at the right time, and you are doing *something* about it.

For now, for this moment, just read the book. And, when you do read it, open your mind and your heart. We wrote it to help you. We wrote it to get you excited. And, we wrote it so that you could have Peace of Mind.

A Message from Bill Quain

July, 2014 – Successful entrepreneurs Jay Tuerk, Yoni Ashurov and Bill Hoffmann had just launched a new company called My Warranty Rewards. Jay and Yoni had been in the Peace of Mind business for some time, creating warranty packages for consumer electronics and automobiles. Warranty packages give people Peace of Mind because they remove the worry about paying for complex products that can fail, resulting in a big bill to replace the defective item.

As an author, I always keep my eyes open for an opportunity to tell a success story and My Warranty Rewards looked like it would be a REAL success. I was introduced to Bill Hoffmann and Jay Tuerk, and we arranged to have a meeting at *Tavern on the Green* restaurant in New York's Central Park. I wanted to learn more about their company, and how they bring Peace of Mind to so many people, at such a low price. I had sent them a book proposal, and we were all looking forward to the process.

But, I was totally unprepared for what happened next. All of a sudden I was presented with the gift that all authors are looking for. I found a topic that was so big, so impressive, and so impactful that it nearly took my breath away. *I had been looking at Peace of Mind in an economic, technological way, and in just a few sentences, Bill Hoffmann completely turned my head around. He was also looking at Peace of Mind — but from an entirely different perspective!*

I remember the moment clearly, because Bill leaned across the table and said, "I don't think this book should be limited to Peace of Mind through warranties. Instead, why don't we show people how to create true Peace of Mind? I am talking about *freedom* here—a basic freedom from the worries of not having enough money to pay the bills, *and* the Freedom to make choices to enjoy life. Isn't that what real Peace of Mind is?"

Okay, I don't know how you would react to this situation. As an author, I was immediately humbled by the opportunity. Real Peace of Mind—freedom from worry—is such a marvelous topic, that the sudden realization that I was dealing with BIG thinking, and that I might have the opportunity to capture that big thinking, was overwhelming. You see, authors only get their hands on a BIG topic like this once or twice in a lifetime.

But guess what? As a person who is reading this book, looking for something as powerful and magnificent as true Peace of Mind, you are sitting in the same seat I was. YOU are on the brink of discovering a secret that could change your family's future. YOU have the opportunity to open your mind to a really powerful idea, and YOU will shortly have the step-by-step instruction on how to make it actually happen!

But, let's not get ahead of ourselves. I want you to do the same thing I did when Bill Hoffmann shared his thoughts on Peace of Mind with me that day, July 11, 2014. I don't want you to suddenly put this book down and shout, "I got it." Instead, do like I did that afternoon. I sat back and started *changing my perspective on the subject.* I let it wash over me for a bit.

Can you take a little time, read this book and *think* about what you are about to learn? And, more importantly, as you see that ordinary men and women can change their lives forever, YOU will have the responsibility to spread that message to others.

I hope that happens to you, just like it happened to me that day. I want you to be humbled by the knowledge you are about to learn. I want you to have the feeling of excitement when you get this news. This isn't just something new. This book isn't about saving some money or getting a great deal (although, you are going to learn about that stuff as well). No, this book is about a change in your life. It is also about the responsibility you are now going to have to spread this word.

You know other people who need Peace of Mind, don't you? You have friends, family members and acquaintances that are stressed out—particularly by financial pressures—who could use this information. People are hurting. They are looking for answers. They are struggling under the weight of worry and fear.

So, welcome to this idea. Welcome to the threshold of a VERY big opportunity to change. Welcome to the beginning of the next chapter in your life—possibly the biggest opportunity you are likely to get on this earth.

This is *the right time, and it is YOUR time.* Read the words of Jay, Yoni and Bill. These are serious guys! They know what they are doing, and they will help you do what is right for you, your family, and anyone who wants to gain Peace of Mind.

Read this book. Believe the message. Pass it on.

𝔓eace of 𝔐ind

Business Times

Bill Hoffmann

Bill Hoffmann can predict the future. His uncanny ability to see what lies ahead tells him network marketing is where smart business needs to be.

"If you, as an entrepreneur, get ahead of the trend and are first to market, there is no competition out there," he said.

A longtime insurance broker who correctly foretold the direction of the telecom and travel industries, Hoffmann teaches agents with My Warranty Rewards the tricks that made him successful. In return, he is rewarded with an income that far exceeds what he earned when he owned his health and life insurance business, and he isn't constantly frustrated by employee turnover.

"I would bring people in, and the really sharp ones would leave after a year or two," he said of his insurance days, which ended in 1994. "They'd go across the street and open up their own business and they'd become my competition."

His options, as he saw it, were to stop hiring astute individuals or stop sharing the methods that had made him wealthy. "Neither made sense to me," he said.

So he turned to network marketing, a concept he calls "the purest form of entrepreneurship."

"Now, I teach others to succeed and I get paid for helping them," Hoffmann said. "They want to be more successful than I was. The better they do, the better I do."

He first used network marketing in the telecom business when deregulation in 1990 opened up the monopoly once held by Ma Bell and again in 2000 when the Travel Industry moved from the traditional agency to online. Through network marketing, he sold online travel agencies to others, helping to build the world's 11th largest online travel business.

He started his own energy/networking business in 2008, and learned valuable lessons as a company owner. "As a member of the corporate team, I saw firsthand the importance of having a unique product."

Bill first learned about Matrix Protection in 2012, when Jay Tuerk called him for advice about starting a network marketing system for the warranty company. While he was excited about Jay's ideas, Hoffmann couldn't see how the warranty business would fit in with his energy company. Over the next few years, however, he kept an eye on Matrix Protection, because he "immediately recognized the value of a plan that protects electronics products for $1 a day."

But, he couldn't figure out how to merge the idea with his energy business.

(Continued)

"I couldn't bridge how the energy people would sell warranties and stay focused on their jobs," he said.

Ironically, Bill's son was in a completely different position. As a college freshman, he saw great value in an affordable plan that protects the staples of dorm life—such as Xboxes, iPads and mini fridges. Bill's son "jumped into the breach" and started building his own business. He was so adept at it that this year he won a cruise in a company contest for being a top salesperson and didn't return for his sophomore year of college, opting instead to continue adding to his six-figure income.

Hoffman didn't need further convincing. In May 2014, he sold his energy company. In June he became executive vice president of My Warranty Rewards, the direct selling arm of Matrix Protection.

"If you listen to my son, I followed him into the business," Hoffmann said. "I did it for one simple reason: My Warranty Rewards is the first to market. Nobody else on the planet is doing this."

Having no competition allows My Warranty Rewards to define the industry and create a strong brand, while attracting people who want to explore the possibility of earning extra income without leaving the comfort of their jobs. "We will get the best agents in the field," he said. "This opportunity is wide open, because we are unique, and we are first."

But that doesn't mean those people won't have to make an effort, Hoffmann said.

"It is called net*work* marketing because it is '*work*'," he said. "It's not called net-lottery marketing or net-you-don't-have-to-do-anything marketing. It is work, but you can leverage yourself and have financial freedom and peace of mind. My Warranty Rewards," he said," represents all of that."

"I saw an incredible opportunity and I couldn't let it go by," said Hoffmann, who retired a decade ago but returned to work within a year. "I saw what was happening in this industry. Where we are headed, what we can do with it, how we can help a lot of people.

"I believe this is the next one. I don't chase the fad. I position myself in front of the trend."

Chapter 1:
Peace of Mind is
FREEDOM!

"For every minute you remain angry, you give up sixty seconds of peace of mind."

—Ralph Waldo Emerson

Peace of Mind is two kinds of FREEDOM.

Freedom **from** some things such as:

- Fear
- Stress
- Threats
- Collapse
- Financial Failure

*It is also FREEDOM **to do** the following:*

- Live where and how you want to live
- Educate your children as you see fit

- Keep a spouse at home with the family
- Take vacations—whenever and wherever you like
- Make a difference in the world—or just in your neighborhood
- Help others

But, you don't get these freedoms without struggle. All freedom is *won*. All freedom is *achieved*.

We are going to show you just how BIG Peace of Mind really is.

True Peace of Mind isn't something you just fall into. You have to pursue Peace of Mind. You have to really want it! Folks, we are talking *Freedom* here.

What is it Like to Have Peace of Mind?

When someone asks us, "What is it like to have Peace of Mind?" we tell them just one thing. It is fantastic! Imagine how good it would feel to be truly at peace. And, we don't mean that you will not have challenges. We don't mean that all the bad stuff in the world (like recessions, health issues, relationship problems, etc.) will suddenly go away. Those things are still out there—just waiting to throw troubles into your life. But, we ARE telling you that true Peace of Mind means that those things will no longer impact you like they used to do.

Imagine this: There is another recession, and another round of layoffs. People are losing their homes. Parents are worried about sending their kids to college. Foreclosures are happening.

But, YOU are not worried, because YOU have done something to prepare for these eventualities. You are still able to pay your bills, and your home is safe. YOUR kids are going to college if they like and YOUR family is still able to take vacations.

If you face a health challenge, YOUR income is still secure. YOUR lifestyle is not threatened, and you have that feeling of security and contentment that comes from being free. You can't stop the illnesses, economic disasters, crazy bosses, and other bad things, but you can make them less important.

You have freedom from worry *in the future,* because you chose to use your FREEDOM TO ACT *now!*

That is what Peace of Mind feels like. It is both freedom from fear and stress AND that great feeling you will get when you look back and say, "I am so glad that I took action!"

Peace of Mind *Isn't* a Thing of the Past

Okay, Peace of Mind is Freedom, but you have to use your Freedom of Choice NOW in order to have Peace of Mind in the future. This is sometimes a difficult concept for people, because they tend to equate Peace of Mind with the past—a simpler time, with fewer complications. This makes it difficult for them to take action now.

You are probably way ahead of us on this part of the topic, right? You may be saying, "Yes, I *do* remember having more Peace of Mind. It was a time when things were simpler and safer. I had fewer responsibilities."

Don't worry, this happens to almost all of us. We get "stuck" in the past as we imagine a time when our bosses couldn't get in touch with us 24 hours a day, or when our kids didn't have to worry about Internet privacy issues, or when… well, you get the picture.

Here is some news: the world is never going to get any simpler. And, to tell you the truth, you don't want to go back to the "good old days." Would you give up ATM machines, your computer and tablet, the ability to stay in touch with your kids, etc.? Personally, we like those things. We can take action more quickly, and resolve problems almost immediately. If we use those technologies correctly, we can keep small things from turning into BIG things.

Yes, Peace of Mind can sometimes live in the past in our minds, but as you read this book we want you to realize that Peace of Mind is a present, and future-thinking concept. You must take action today (using your Freedom of Choice) in order to have Peace of Mind in the future.

And always remember this: you can't change the world. You can only change yourself. Use your Freedom of Choice to change the things you can change. Prepare to have Peace of Mind by making some changes now.

Peace of Mind is "Achievement not Acceptance"

One of the largest obstacles to Peace of Mind is that you might be waiting for someone to *give* you something, rather than actively going after it. It is an easy trap to fall into. We are *taught* to wait for things in our life. "Be patient," they say. "Don't force the issue," they tell us.

What have you been waiting for and what have you been accepting?

- You waited for teachers to teach you the things you needed to know. Each year, they doled out a little more. They told you what the right answers were, and how to get those answers. If you came up with another answer, they told you that you were wrong and took away your grade.

- You waited for your boss to give you a raise, and accepted whatever she gave you. But when you have to accept what they give you, you will never get what you need, and you will CERTAINLY not get what you deserve.

- You waited for someone to recognize your worth—whether it was at work or at school. But often, someone else would get the praise, the promotion or the recognition.

Folks, you probably have spent a lifetime waiting for something, and then been forced to accept the absolute *average* that everyone else gets. When you are so busy waiting and then accepting, you miss out on all the truly outstanding opportunities that are presented to you.

No One Gives You Peace of Mind

Let's be clear—attaining Peace of Mind is your responsibility.

No one is going to give you something so exceptional. The system is just not set up that way. Your teachers, your boss, the government, EVERYTHING is set up to make you average, keep you average, and keep everyone around you average. Average is BAD! The average family in the United States has over $7,000 in credit card debt that they will NEVER pay off. The average family is just three paychecks away from being completely broke. The average person is living in stress, fear and doubt.

Yes, the world is willing to give you an *average* life. But, if you want something more, then you must go out and get it. That is quite an achievement, and besides the Peace of Mind it brings you financially, it is one of the greatest feelings of accomplishment that you will ever have.

So, How do You ACHIEVE Peace of Mind?

There are five steps:

1. Decide that you WANT Peace of Mind.
2. Learn to think differently about Peace of Mind.
3. Apply the 80/20 rule (you'll learn this soon) and prioritize your needs.
4. Find a vehicle that gives you Peace of Mind without disrupting your life. (Read On!)
5. Take action and seek Peace of Mind. Achieve it through your own initiative. (However, if you choose the right vehicle, you will enjoy the support of a great team! Again, read on.)

Finally, after deciding that you want Peace of Mind, and you start thinking differently about it, we can show you the steps to achieve it—for yourself and for your family.

Always remember this: we are going to make it easy for you. You will *achieve* your Peace of Mind by helping other people *achieve* theirs. And this is important: you will never have to face this challenge alone. You will be a member of a team, and that team will be there to support you. But unlike teams you may be involved with right now, you are never going to be held back by your team. If you want more, you can get more.

No one is going to ask you to wait for something. You will not be expected to remain "average." We are going to encourage you to live in the present, and to use your Freedom of Choice to *direct* your life. We expect you to achieve something great, because we know you are capable of doing just that.

Congratulations, you are right on the brink of achieving something very special. Never accept anything less ever again.

Chapter 2:
Your Peace of Mind Checklist: Applying the 80/20 Rule

*"I advise you to say your dream is possible
and then overcome all inconveniences,
ignore all the hassles, and take a running leap
through the hoop even if it is in flames."*

—Les Brown, Author and Speaker

What Would Peace of Mind Look Like For You?

Now, we realize that everyone is different, and everyone has particular things they like and don't like. But, here are some broad ideas of what most people would think of as Peace of Mind:

1. Your family is happy and healthy.

2. You have enough money to pay your bills and do the things you would like to do (vacations, nice car, college tuitions, help loved ones).

3. You have the time to enjoy life.

4. You do something meaningful and fulfilling. (Make a contribution that people recognize as important.)

5. You receive recognition for your achievements.

6. You continuously associate with great people who respect you and want to be around you.

7. You and your loved ones are safe.

These aren't all of the Peace of Mind factors of course, but let's face it—if you had this kind of life, it would be a lot better than what you have now, right? Wouldn't these things give you remarkable Peace of Mind?

Watch Out for Disrupters

What are Disrupters? They are the things that suddenly come into your life and wreck your Peace of Mind. They could be complicated, global things like a world-wide economic crisis. But, they are much more likely to be simple, yet highly annoying and frustrating things like a boss who "comes up with a great idea." (You know the kind of idea we mean, don't you? It is one like, "Why don't we all work through the weekend to catch up on these reports?")

Disrupters *disrupt* your hard-earned Peace of Mind. They make your life stressful. Did you get a sudden and unexpected bill? This is a disrupter! Did your kid just fall and chip two front teeth? Right again—a disrupter.

Here is the important thing you need to remember about disrupters. You can't *prevent* them, but you can certainly *anticipate* them and build up your resources so that they have less impact on your life. This is the secret to Peace of Mind—*doing something now so that the disrupters will not impact your life later.*

A Big Problem—Trying to Get Rid of Disrupters is Disrupting!!!

You don't have any spare time, do you? So, when we start talking about disrupters in your life, you say, "Yes, I know I have a bunch of stuff going on. But, if you are going to give me a complicated system for getting RID of those things, I will just sit down and cry." We understand. You *get* our basic point—you need to get rid of disrupters in order to have Peace of Mind—but you need something that isn't disruptive itself. Well, guess what? You are in luck. We are about to share a simple system that will give you a laser-focus mindset. This system will clear up all the clutter and help you work ONLY on the things that are going to make a difference. More importantly, you can *forget* the other stuff.

How do You Eat an Elephant? One Bite at a Time!

If so many people do NOT have Peace of Mind, why don't they do something about it?

---

1. Most people don't know how to get started.
2. They try to do everything all at once.

We see it all the time. Someone decides to make a change in his/her life, and then they are suddenly overwhelmed. For example, how many people fail at their #1 New Year's resolution: losing weight?

Too many sudden changes are the problem: "I won't eat sweets," "I'll go to the gym every day," "I won't order lunch at work," "I'll take the stairs instead of the elevator," "I can't go off my diet even one day."

But, it doesn't happen, does it? One of the BIG reasons people fail is that we try to do everything all at once.

What does This Have to do with Peace of Mind?

Ironically, trying to *gain* Peace of Mind is like trying to *lose* weight. You are not going to get out of your crazy, frantic, complicated, and debt-ridden life overnight, and you are not going to lose weight all in one day either.

You can't just make a resolution and then expect your life to change—just because you said it should. You have to do some work to get Peace of Mind. You have to look at the BIG picture and give it some time. You need to set some goals, some dreams, and work on each one of them.

And most importantly, you need to do something that works: works for you and makes you happy while you do it.

So how do you do that? You follow the 80/20 Rule.

The 80/20 Rule

Have you ever heard of The 80/20 Rule? It says:

Eighty percent of the rewards come from twenty percent of the things you do.

Eighty percent of the problems come from just twenty percent of what you do.

Eighty percent of the rewards come from just twenty percent of your effort.

Is The 80/20 Rule scientifically proven? Of course not, but most people, and we are some of those people, believe that it applies to most things in life. It certainly applies to your Peace of Mind—or your *lack of Peace of Mind.*

Try this part of The 80/20 Rule:
If you changed just 20% of the things you are doing wrong now, you would have 80% of the Peace of Mind you deserve!

In other words, if you change the right things in your life, you can get HUGE rewards that are beyond proportion to the small amount of work you actually do. If you apply your effort to correct 20% of the factors in your life that are causing you problems, you can eliminate 80% of the problems.

Folks, this one principle, The 80/20 Rule, *is so powerful that you can make massive, PERMANENT changes in your life—fast.*

Your 80/20 Rule Checklist

Okay, fasten your seat belts, because this is a secret that almost NO ONE knows about. It works because it will help you to organize all the seemingly random information that is flying around you into a simple checklist. You can do this in a weekend, and make a difference for the rest of your life!

We call this "Comment Card Analysis." It is based on the comment cards you see all over the place. For example, if you go into a restaurant, they may ask you to fill out a comment card. You are asked to rate the service, the food, etc. And, you are invited to write down a comment or two at the end.

Well, we want YOU to fill out comment cards about **YOURSELF**! It's so simple and you'll be amazed at the results.

Chapter 3:
Gaining Peace of Mind—Without Losing It!

"I am thankful the most important key in history was invented. It's not the key to your house, your car, your boat, your safe deposit box, your bike lock or your private community. It's the key to order, sanity and peace of mind. The key is 'Delete.'"

—Elayne Boosler

The 80/20 rule helps you find the things that are having the greatest negative impact and then work on those things first. This enables you to put your effort into the high-impact areas—the ones that are causing you the most problems. And, you will often find that once you have solved the biggest problems, the smaller ones go away as well. This is how successful people work.

So, how does this apply to you and your Peace of Mind? It is very simple. Just follow these steps:

1. Make a list of comments about the negative things in your life. (This is just like filling out a personal comment card.)

2. Sort the comments into Categories.

3. Determine which Category has the BIGGEST impact on your Peace of Mind and concentrate ONLY on that Category.

You need to make a list of the disrupters in your life, and then put them into categories.

How do I Get Started?

Here is an example of what we did in an afternoon. We started calling up people we know and asking them, "What things disrupt your Peace of Mind?" Now, it took a little explaining, because they had not read the book, and they had never heard of "disrupters". But, after a little explaining, they started to open up and talk!

They had lots to say, and it wasn't long until we had 100 comments that our friends told us were disrupting their Peace of Mind. All we did was write them down. We put them into an Excel spreadsheet on the computer, and started breaking them into categories. (You don't need a computer. Just make a list and count!)

Categories? What Categories?

After looking over the 100 comments, we discovered five categories that made sense for almost all of the comments. These categories are:

1. Financial (with two subsets – "employment" and "property")

2. Health

3. Family/Relationships

4. Legal/Technological

5. Self-Worth/Self-Image

Once we had the list of comments completed, we simply assigned the corresponding number of the category to each comment. For example, we assigned the comment, "After working all day, I am too tired to shop for food or cook," to Category #1 (Financial) because we put anything to do with career and employment under the Financial Category.

Note: The complete list of all the comments, along with the category number that each one was assigned to, is available at the back of this book in Appendix A. (You will want to use this list when you do your own Comment List.)

After assigning each comment to a category, we simply added up the number of comments in each category, and using our spreadsheet software, we created two charts: a bar chart showing the number of comments in each category, and a pie chart showing the percentages. These charts are below:

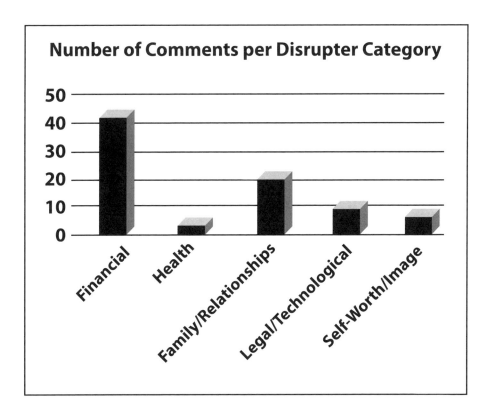

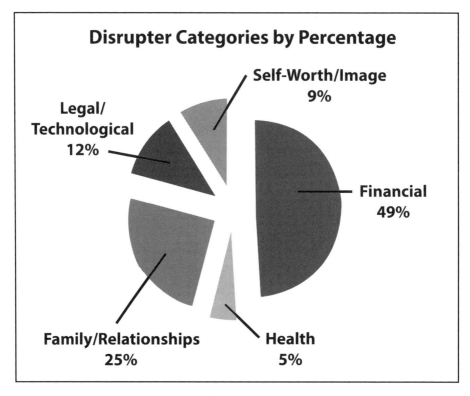

A quick look at these two charts indicates that *Financial* disrupters were the most common in this sample (49 comments out of 100, or 49% of the total disrupter comments). The next most impactful category was *Family/Relationships* (25 comments and 25% of total disrupters).

Our Advice to this Person?

Now, suppose this was just one person's set of comments, instead of a summary from a number of people. What advice would we give this person? More importantly, if this were *YOU*, what advice would you give yourself?

Where would your time and effort be likely to yield the biggest results?

Overcoming the Financial disrupters in your life would yield the biggest impact.

It is simple, isn't it? In this case, the Financial Disrupters were causing the biggest problems for this person. Solving one problem—the Financial Problem—would solve 49% of all the problems this person faces. And, think about this. Some of the comments that were listed as "Family/Relationship" could easily be a result of financial challenges. For example, we listed "My child was sick and I couldn't get off from work," as a Family/Relationship comment, but if this person was financially independent, or at least, was not so dependent upon her job that she couldn't get a little time off to take care of her child, she would not have this particular disrupter upsetting her Peace of Mind.

Do I Have to Attack the Biggest Disrupters First?

This is a good question, and the answer depends on how serious you are about getting Peace of Mind! Remember, one of the things that is driving you crazy—paralyzing you and overwhelming you—is that you are trying to fix everything at once. STOP! Give yourself a break! Put your effort where it will do the most good.

In the case above, we would recommend that this person should start to look for ways to start making more money, without spending too much time doing it. For example, we would NOT recommend that she/he take on another job. We would NOT recommend another commute, or doing something that MUST be done during certain hours of the day. This person needs to develop a second source of income that is *flexible* and *residual*. And, she/he needs to start working on this QUICKLY. (Using Freedom of Choice today, in order to have Peace of Mind tomorrow.)

What Should I do Now?

Here is our suggestion. Take a look at the list of comments we have in Appendix A. Using them, make your own list. Cross out the ones that do not apply to you, and write in some others that you think are important. You should still have a list of about 100 comments, because this is what you will get when you examine your current situation.

Everyone's list will be a little different. Everyone has his or her own special challenges. But, don't let one or two comments overwhelm you. For example, if you are sick, or chronically ill, don't get too focused on that one thing. Write down *everything* that is disrupting your Peace of Mind.

We advise you to use the five categories listed in this example. Why make more work for yourself? This isn't an exercise in a detailed examination of your life. It is merely a way to get a bird's-eye view of what ails you!

But, I Don't Know How to Use a Spreadsheet

Don't let this be an excuse. Just write the comments on a piece of paper and count the categories by hand. Draw your graph on a plain piece of paper. The important thing is to take the opportunity to do this.

Summary

Okay, let's look at this chapter and put it all together. You need to prioritize your time and effort, and you need to stop trying to solve every problem every day. It is just too much for you.

1. **Make a list** of all the things that are keeping you from enjoying Peace of Mind in this life. It won't take long. In fact, once you get started, it goes very quickly.

2. **Divide the comments into categories**, and make a "picture" of the results by creating charts like the Bar Chart and Pie Chart we showed in this chapter. And, we do suggest that you put this picture somewhere that is plainly visible. Keep your charts in front of you.

3. **Choose your category!** Get to work on the biggest problem. Don't sweat the small stuff.

Will We Help You?

Of course! In fact, we are about to unveil a plan to help almost everyone overcome his or her problems in the most common "high-impact" category—the Financial Category. What about the other categories, *Health and Family/Relationships*? Don't worry, if you solve the Financial Category you will be so full of Peace of Mind that your other challenges will soon be a distant memory as well.

Will it work every time? Will it work for everyone? Well, we can't promise that it will work for you, but we can promise this: <u>*We will work for you to help you gain your Peace of Mind*</u>!

Are you ready?

𝔓𝔢𝔞𝔠𝔢 𝔬𝔣 𝔐𝔦𝔫𝔡

Business Times

Jay Tuerk—The Man with the Disrupting Plan

Jay Tuerk is an expert on warranties and he's looking to revolutionize the industry. Consumed by a passion to serve the consumer, Tuerk has created Matrix Protection, a program that allows consumers to protect all their household devices for $1 a day. His plan is to eliminate the need for consumers to purchase warranties, also known as extended service agreements, in stores.

"Warranties were never created for the consumer," Tuerk said. "They were started for the retailers to pump their profits up. The consumer is the last on the totem pole."

To Tuerk, that kind of thinking is backward. The consumer should come first, and the only way that will happen is if the consumer has an alternative to the high-pressure, over-priced warranties peddled by brick-and-mortar stores. Enter Matrix Protection, a plan that allows consumers to insure any electronics they have bought, up to four years prior to signing up with Matrix, and any electronics they will buy in the future, for $29.97 a month.

"We wanted to create a program that encompasses all the electronics in the home under one umbrella agreement," Tuerk said. "We made it affordable and took out all the extra profit retailers make. It makes sense for consumers to protect all the stuff they have and all stuff they're going to have."

Tuerk has been in the warranty business since 1974, and said it is virtually the same now as it was 40 years ago.

"People don't understand the business," he said. "They don't know what price they should pay. What makes all of this crazier is they'll pay $225 for a TV warranty for a couple of years, a warranty that maybe the retailer paid $30 for, and they'll pay for it with a credit card. That adds insult to injury, paying for the over-bloated warranty with a credit card. Who knows when they're going to pay that off?"

The automobile industry is one of the biggest offenders, Tuerk said, inflating car payments by an extra $80 to $135 per month through the sale of expensive warranties.

"Depending upon how weak you are and how strong they are, you're going to spend another $3,000 to $4,000 on an auto warranty," he said. "You go into a little room, the door closes, the shutter comes down, the air conditioning goes off, and those guys are going to sweat you out because they get paid a percentage of what they sell."

Tuerk doesn't do business that way, and with the evolution of shopping already under way, sees no need to.

"The industry is not going to change," he said. "The big shift going on now *(Continued)* is in the way people buy products because of the Internet. People go to the store, get the model number of the TV they want to buy, and go home and order it online. Stores are becoming showrooms, so now they're really desperate for the warranty sale. They need the warranty sales to survive."

Purchasing warranties piece by piece is disorganized and inefficient, Tuerk said. Matrix Protection simplifies the management of all the technological devices a consumer owns by listing all the products with the same insurer. There are no tricky rate charts. The cost of protection is not a percentage based on the purchase price of the product, as traditional warranties are. There is one flat fee and no limit on the number of electronics that can be enrolled in the plan.

Planned obsolescence—the built-in timeframe a device stops working just as the manufacturer's warranty expires—is a driving force in the sales of extended warranties. Tuerk said consumers do not have to keep warranties they no longer need or want.

"If you already have a warranty on your car or TV, cancel it," he said. "You'll get a pro-rated portion of the price back. Nobody's going to tell you that, but you can cancel at any time. It's the law."

He is aiming, he said, "to create a movement" using network marketing to "flood the country with independent agents." By merging traditional business with network marketing, Tuerk said his company has found the synergy to attract quality people to promote a warranty program that, finally, puts the consumer first.

"We don't care about the retailer or dealer," Tuerk said. "My job is to build a program that is exactly what the consumer needs, and to do it at a fair profit."

7 Things You Probably DID NOT KNOW About Warranties

1. Although we call them *warranties* throughout this book, they are actually *Extended Service Contracts, Extended Warranties*, or *Protection Plans*.

2. By law, you can cancel almost any warranty (Extended Service Contract) and get your pro-rated money back! For example, if you just paid $225 to protect a new computer, and now you want to switch your protection to Matrix Protection, you can do it. (By the way, Bill Quain discovered this also works for car warranties— even if the car is totaled in an accident!)

3. Most retailers and car dealers sell warranties because they don't make much money on the actual products they sell. A computer warranty that costs the customer $225 might only cost the retailer $35—a profit of $190. And a car warranty that sells for $3,000 might only cost the car dealer $400.

4. Most retailers and car dealers do NOT own the warranty. Instead, another company called a "Third Party Administrator" creates the warranty, prints a brochure with the name of the retailer or car dealer on it, and then services the warranty. The retailer/dealer only has a minor role in the warranty process. What is that role? *Selling you the warranty and putting a fat profit into their bank account.*

5. Almost all retailers and car dealers *train their people* to sell, sell, and sell warranties. In Big Box Retailers, even the CASHIERS are trained to sell warranties. Why? Because of all the profits those warranties create.

6. There is a "Gotcha" moment in all transactions, when the retailer or dealer is *trained, poised and ready* to sell you a warranty. It is when you have just made the purchase decision, and you

have your credit card out, (electronics) or are about to sign the final agreement (car). At this point, you have just made a decision to spend a lot of money, and you are thinking, "I need to protect my investment."

7. *ALL* warranties are backed by insurance and those insurance companies know *EXACTLY* how long your new product is expected to last. Most warranty plans are designed to END just before you really need them. NOTE: Extended Warranty plans are like the odds at a casino. Over time, the house always wins, because the house (the retailer/car dealership) is playing the odds!

Finally, you can stop overpaying, get Peace of Mind, avoid the "gotcha moment" and save hundreds, and maybe thousands of dollars by using the Matrix Protection Suite of Products. These are *lifetime* extended warranties. Wouldn't it be nice if the warranty actually outlived the product?

Chapter 4:
An Industry Turned Upside Down—Or, How to Make Money by Shaking It Out of the Big *Box*

"An organization's ability to learn, and translate that learning into action rapidly, is the ultimate competitive advantage."

—Jack Welch

Every now and again, an industry becomes so greedy and old-fashioned that it opens the door to new ideas—and throws off huge profits to the people who seize that opportunity. The Warranty Industry is in that position right now—and YOU are in the position to walk through that open door of opportunity.

Folks, this business is really very simple. It has all the elements necessary for you to do well—very well. You don't need to know much about the business itself because My Warranty Rewards is doing all the heavy lifting. You just need to understand a few basic facts about the industry, and more importantly, you need to understand how and why people seek security, certainty and service.

The first part—a few facts about the industry—will be easy to teach you because you already have a lot of experience with this business. After all, you have either been offered a warranty, or you have purchased a warranty dozens of times in your lifetime. The second part—teaching you how and why people buy warranties for protection and security is also something you know quite a bit about.

So, buckle your seat belts and get ready to make some interesting, and profitable discoveries. This fruit is ready to be plucked!

Why is the Warranty Business Upside Down?

Here is the simple answer:

The traditional warranty business was created to make retailers more profitable, not to make consumers more secure.

That is all you need to know in order to get really excited about this business. Any time a product is meant to serve *only* the person who is going to make money on it, it presents a wide-open door for even the simplest person to walk through and make money. Consumers *hate* being ripped off. They don't want their money to go to a store that is delivering them a bad deal. It may take a while, but eventually, consumers catch on. And when they do, watch out!

Let's look at a typical Warranty transaction and see if it is designed to protect consumers, or to make money for the store. Let's say that our friend Joe decides to buy a new computer. He pays $700 for the computer, and when he reaches the cash register, just as he takes out his credit card from the safety of his wallet, the clerk says, "Joe, that fine machine I have been telling you about is fantastic. I know you are going to love it. But to tell you the truth, the entire thing may blow up and disintegrate at any moment—especially in the first three years. But, our store doesn't want you to suffer, so we can offer you a fantastic, bumper-to-bumper *protection plan* for just $225. Every smart person who bought that computer, which like I said, is likely to blow up in your face at any time, was also smart enough to protect themselves against the almost certain violent and unexpected demise of that machine. Would you like to get two or three years of coverage—just so that your family does not suffer too much when the unthinkable happens?"

Does this sound familiar? It should, every clerk and cash register jockey in every retail store that sells electronics, or appliances, or automobiles, is *trained and re-trained* to make a forceful pitch to you when you are at your most vulnerable. And, when is that specific time? You guessed it, when you are standing there with your credit card out, and all you can now think about is the almost-certain disruption of your life when that darned thing emits a sudden cloud of smoke and maybe even a deep sigh of resignation, just as you are about to press the "save" button.

And, it isn't even the fact that you will be out your $700 that you just paid out of your pocket, you will also be kicking yourself for not buying the warranty when it does happen! Even worse, if you are married, it will be your spouse who will be kicking you. Your kids will kick you. Your friends will say, "Joe, you are an idiot. Why didn't you buy that protection plan from the nice sales clerk when he/she offered it to you at such a wonderful price? Yes, it would have cost the equivalent of one-fourth of the total cost, but I'll bet you are sorry NOW!"

Talk about *vulnerable*. You don't want to spend the money on that warranty. In fact, you didn't want to spend the money on the item you are buying. You just wanted to have something that did some sort of job for you. You just wanted to do word processing, or watch movies, or drive it, or listen to it. That's all you wanted.

But NO, those salespeople wanted something different. They wanted your money—even though you were buying a warranty at a price that far exceeds the benefits you are going to get, if the product ever needs to be repaired or replaced.

Why do They do This to Us?

The retailers didn't make enough money on the stuff they sold you.

They won't stay in business selling computers, televisions, or even cars at the minuscule profit margins that today's retail environment allows. You see, the retail store, and even the retail car dealerships, are competing with the Internet. Take a store like Best Buy for example. How much can they possibly make on a computer that you can easily get online for a lower price?

Today, you can use the Big Box retailer (or car dealership) as a showroom only experience. You can find out exactly what you want and do not want, research the prices at other stores while you are standing there (using your smart phone) and then walk out of the store and order it all online!

The retailers know this. They cut their prices so low that there is very little profit left. How much do they make on a $700 computer? We don't know, but we bet it isn't much. And, they have to pay employees, build the warehouse and store, stock it all with expensive merchandise, advertise and offer coupons, keep everything clean and deal with shoplifters.

They have to do all that, and then they have to sell everything at almost zero profit—to someone like you who just walks in there and simply *looks* at what they have and never buys it directly from them! How would you like to be in that business?

So, they come up with things to sell you that have almost no cost to them, and they never have to worry about competition. They make up a product that is simple, low-cost, and is almost pure profit, and then they do everything in their power to sell it to you, whether it is the best thing for you as a consumer or not.

They have been to training class after training class to learn EXACTLY what trigger words to use on you. They are waiting there, for just the minute you whip out that credit card. When they see it begin to slide out of your wallet, they kick it into overdrive—not to protect you, but to make more money (and in many cases, to keep their jobs).

And that is why this industry is upside down. From start to finish, from top to bottom, everything is geared towards making more money for the retailers.

Folks, when you see a situation like this, you have to say to yourself, "What if someone DID find a way to make these warranties a true protection for the consumers? Is it possible?"

Well, it is more than possible—it is here!

Don't Miss the BIGGEST Clue of All!

Look, we wouldn't be telling you that there is an upside-down industry where you could make money by changing the focus from the retailer to the consumer if there wasn't one big thing in that market—DEMAND! You see, despite the bad deal that these made-for-retailers-and-not-for-consumers warranties actually represent, MILLIONS of them are sold each year, to MILLIONS of customers who actually want these warranties.

These customers are looking for one thing—Peace of Mind.

And, they actually believe they are getting it. They are willing to buy even more warranties. They want to be protected, and they want to alleviate the stress of having to worry about a large investment going "whoosh" in a ball of flame. And finally, they don't want to look stupid in front of their spouses, children and friends when that thing has to be repaired or replaced.

Warranties are actually a good thing—but only if the consumer gets a fair shake.

Want More Proof that Warranties are Made for Retailers?

Here is a simple story. Mary Jo buys a smart phone for her daughter. Mary Jo also buys two warranties—one against product and manufacturer defects, and one against the certain day when her daughter is trying to put on makeup and use the phone at the same time, dropping the phone on the cement driveway—two stories below the open window where she is sitting because, "the natural light is great up there." Of course, the daughter also just took off her old phone case because she wanted to change to a different color. She has not bought the new case yet.

The warranty will cover the cost to repair the phone's shattered screen. However, there is one problem: Mary Jo does not remember if she has a warranty for that kind of damage, and if she does, she certainly does not know where the receipt is, or how to activate the warranty claim. In fact, the company that sold Mary Jo the phone is no longer selling phones. The store is now a nail polish salon.

Folks, if a warranty were made for consumers, there would be some easy way for consumers to use it! But, there isn't, is there?

Even if you bought the phone from a Big Box retailer, and that retailer is still in business, the retailer has absolutely NOTHING to do with the warranty once it is sold in the store. No, the nice clerk at the store (you can't remember her name, but she was wearing a blue shirt the day you bought the phone) cannot help you. A third party administers the warranty. It turns out that the store is only marginally involved in the entire warranty process. (How are they *marginally* involved? Simple, they are increasing their profit *margins* of course!)

And Another Thing…

If warranties were really made for consumers, and not retailers, there would be some way to put all your items under one warranty, right?

Instead of having to pay all that money every time you buy a new item, wouldn't a consumer-friendly warranty plan that lets you put ALL the items you buy under one plan make more sense and save you money by not charging you extra every time you bought more stuff?

Not Quite Convinced? Think About this One

Almost no retailer has its own warranty plan. None of the Big Box stores do. Most auto retailers do not. They all buy their plans from someone else. That "someone else" is called a warranty agency. Warranty agencies create the warranties and then sell them to retailers so the retailers can make more money.

Do these warranty Agents sell directly to the consumer? No, because their products are not made for consumers.

Here is how they sell them. A warranty agency comes up with a warranty program, and then their sales force goes out to big retailers, finds their home offices, walk in and say, "Hi, I am from the _____ warranty agency. I want to show you a great program that will cost you almost nothing, and will make you a bundle. You will not have to deal with those messy customers who have all sorts of crazy problems after they actually buy that almost-no-profit stuff you are selling to them. No, if they have a problem, we will take care of it. All you need to do is to make sure that all your clerks sell this program."

Now, each of these agencies is competing with every other agency that wants to sell warranty programs to the retailers. So, the agencies reduce their prices as much as possible, and perform as many services as possible to make sure their retail customers never have to deal with a customer. After all, they are *selling* to these retailers. They have to come up with a benefits package that appeals to the *retailers*. And, this benefits package focuses on two things: low costs and no hassles.

How Low are the Costs?

A computer or television warranty that sells for $225 to the consumer might cost the retailer about $30. A car warranty that might sell for $3,000 could cost the dealership as little as $400.

At these cost ranges, could the retailer sell them to you for less? Absolutely! Are they about to do that? No, positively not. Why not? That would wreck the only good thing going on in retail today! They don't have to lower their warranty prices because you can't buy a warranty on their stuff anywhere else!

That's right, no Big Box to Big Box warranty transfers. If you buy a computer in Best Buy, you can only get your warranty from Best Buy. (And, to hear them tell it, you can only buy it "right now" while your credit card is just hanging out there, ready to leap out of your hand.)

Enough is Enough, You Convinced Me!

Okay, you can see what we mean when we say, "The Warranty Industry is upside down," right? And, you can see where there is an excellent opportunity to take advantage of that fact, right?

Folks, when this situation exists—a HUGE, ONGOING and GROWING consumer demand for a product—coupled with the fact that the current product/service is absolutely terrible for consumers, then this presents an opportunity.

But, you are just one person. You don't know anything about this industry. On the other hand, you do know that you want to make some more money. *So, all you have to do now is to discover if there is some kind of company out there that is poised to absolutely SMASH this market.* You then have to determine if this company will help you to SMASH the market with them. You need to find a company and a situation that reduces your risk while maximizing your opportunity.

Of course you know that the company is My Warranty Rewards. You have their book.

And now, you have the insight to make the money you need by shaking out the upside down market.

Chapter 5:
Warranty Math—Or, Why Pay More for Less?

"There is only one boss. The customer. And he can fire everybody in the company from the chairman on down, simply by spending his money somewhere else."

—Sam Walton

A gorilla walks into a bar and orders a martini. The bartender is surprised, but decides to serve him anyway. When he put down the drink in front of his guest, the bartender decides to see just how much the gorilla will pay for the martini. "That will be fifty dollars," he said.

The gorilla looked shocked, but paid the fifty dollars. Shortly after finishing his drink, the gorilla got up to leave the bar. As the great ape started to leave, the bartender said, "I am sorry to see you go. We don't get many gorillas in here."

"I am not surprised," said the gorilla. "Fifty bucks is too much for a martini!"

What does this story have to do with Warranty Math? Simple. The gorilla knew that fifty dollars was too much money to charge for a martini for just one reason. You see, the gorilla knew he could buy a martini for a lot less money somewhere else.

But, the same is not true for warranties.

Up until now, you could generally only buy a warranty where you purchased the product you wished to protect.

Folks, if you want to be smarter than a gorilla, read this chapter and find out why you should be saying, "No thanks. That is too much money for a warranty I can get for a lot less."

The Old Math of Warranties

Let's look at the example of Jeanne Quain and her purchase of a new computer. She paid about $600 and the three-year warranty was about $225. Some experts in the warranty business estimate that the warranty cost the Big Box retailer about $30 to purchase, leaving the retailer with a profit of about $195. The experts estimate that this is more than the Big Box retailer made on the *sale of the computer itself.* (No one knows if these numbers are accurate, but the experts agree that they are close.)

The Quains did not purchase the warranty because it was too high a percentage of the total price ($225/$600 = 37%). In addition, the $225 warranty, spread over three years of coverage, would have cost $75/year ($225/3 years = $75 per year). This was just too much money to pay for a warranty on a $600 item. The risk/reward ratio was just too off balance for the Quains to justify the expense.

The Quains still *wanted* a warranty. They know that computers can fail. In fact, they were buying this computer because Jeanne's old computer had failed. The Quains would have purchased the warranty at a better price.

But, there was another reason why they did not buy this warranty. They have three more computers at home, four tablets, three smart phones, and a slew of other electronic devices. Some of the tablets (iPads) cost about $700 each. The phones were also expensive. If the Quains bought warranties for ALL of these valuable items, they would be spending a FORTUNE on warranties.

For example, if they protected the four computers, four iPads, and three smart phones and they paid an average of $75/year for each one of them, their total bill for the year would be $825 (11 items x $75/item/year). And, this would leave many other items not covered by warranty.

Here is another thing that stopped the family from making the warranty purchase. They had just paid out $600 for the computer. Now, they were looking at paying an additional $225—all at once, and all at the same time!

And, they might have put the warranty on their credit card, and ended up paying even MORE money for it. According to an analysis of government data, the average American family owes $7,221 on their credit cards. (Most of which they are never going to pay off.) Instead, they just make the minimum payment each month. How much does a warranty cost when you are paying for it for a lifetime?

Finally, what would happen in three years? NONE of those items would be protected in three years when the warranties ran out. Yes, the warranty agency would send them a nice, official-looking brochure inviting them to renew the warranties, but what would the *new* prices be like on three-year-old machines?

NEW Warranty Math

Bill and Jeanne did not buy the warranty on her computer, but they still wanted an extended service plan that would protect them from having to pay hundreds of dollars unexpectedly. (Well, let's face it. This wouldn't be an *unexpected* expenditure. Those things FAIL from time to time.) Fortunately, they learned about Matrix Protection. They get the coverage they want, at a fraction of the cost. AND, they know what it is going to cost them in the future.

Here is the math:

The Quains actually identified 22 items that could be covered under Matrix Protection. Besides the 11 items listed above, they had televisions sets (at their primary home AND their second home). There were cameras, iPods, printers, Apple TVs, and other devices. The Quains were actually *shocked* to discover how many items they had that qualified for the Matrix Protection plan. How much did they pay for ALL OF THESE ITEMS?

Just $29.97/month. This came out to be about $1. 36 per month/per item ($1.36 x 22 items = $29.97/month).

This is a fantastic savings, but more importantly, it is an *affordable and fair* price to pay for complete coverage of all the electronic items in the Quains' households.

There are some other advantages to paying $29.97/month for all this protection and Peace of Mind. Most people can pay off the cost of the warranty each month without incurring credit card debt. And, the actual value of the coverage increases the longer they hold the coverage. Finally, they can cover ANY item that is less than four years old and falls into the covered categories. Now this is math that the Quains—and YOU—can live with! Stop overpaying for warranties. Get Peace of Mind for about $1/day and buy your Peace of Mind at a bargain price.

Chapter 6:

The Average Joe and His Search for Warranty Peace of Mind

"Empty pockets never held anyone back. Only empty heads and empty hearts can do that."

—Norman Vincent Peale

The average person knows almost nothing about the structure and function of the Warranty Industry. We know this because WE are average people and WE did not know how the industry worked until Jay Tuerk revealed it to us! So, to get a good idea of what is really going on, let's start by sharing what the average person is thinking right now.

Our "average person" is named Joe. He has a wife (Mary Jo) and two kids, (Joe Jr. and Beth). *Author's Note:* Yes, we know these are pretty common names, but remember, this is an "average" guy!

Joe and Mary Jo have the things you need in today's world. They each have a car, a smart phone, laptop and a tablet. The kids have phones, laptops, tablets, and electronic game equipment. In other words, they are an average family, just trying to get along in today's world.

Joe and Mary Jo understand that the family members all need to have decent electronics, because the world has changed substantially. The kids need the stuff to keep up in school and the parents need it for work. And, the whole family likes to stay connected.

Even the cars that Joe and Mary Jo drive are dependent on technology. For example, the couple uses GPS to save time, follow directions, and find a nearby restaurant.

But the new technology in cars has made it difficult for Joe to do simple repairs and tune-ups. And when there is a repair problem, the bill is likely to be a lot higher than it used to be.

In other words, this family, like all modern families, is completely dependent on technology that did not exist a few years ago. This technology makes their lives better and more effective, but it also comes with a price—a BIG price. It costs *money* to keep all this technology running and performing, and it takes *money* to buy all this technology.

The Cost of Our "Stuff"

There are five essential "costs" that Joe and Mary Jo, and all families in the U.S. will face. Here they are:

1. Purchase—This stuff is not cheap! And, it didn't exist just a few years ago. Take a look at the list of technologies that Joe and Mary Jo's family possesses. They have four smart phones, plus four laptops and lots of other stuff. How much does your family have invested in technology? (Hey, don't forget the cars!)

2. Ongoing costs—If you have a smart phone and/or a tablet/laptop, you probably have a data plan. *Of course* you have an Internet plan and a cable bill at home. These costs are frightening, aren't they? Your car needs maintenance every three thousand miles.

3. Upgrade costs—Is it any accident that tech companies release "new and improved" gadgets every year or so? Of course not. The new models are faster, but they are also expensive.

4. Repair costs—Look, this stuff breaks! It may be a product failure, or it may be an accident, but you have to expect to make repairs to these things. It should be in your budget.

5. Replacement—If a product cannot be repaired, or if you simply lose it, you will have to replace it or miss out on the enjoyment or assistance that technology gave you. Again, you should be budgeting these replacement costs, because you are going to need that money at some time.

How Does the Average Joe Manage These Costs?

Well, the *average* Joe doesn't do a very good job at it at all. He (or she—as in Mary Jo) makes decisions based on need and then hopes for the best. For example, Joe/Mary Jo decides it is time for a new computer: the old one may have stopped working, it's too slow, it was stolen, or they just like the look of the newest models.

Whatever the reason, the couple goes to the store and looks over the available laptops. It is at this point that some interesting things start to happen. Most people begin to look for the LEAST expensive machine that will do what they want it to do. Often times, that least expensive machine is last year's model, with a limited amount of storage space, and a slower than average processor. Why does the couple look for this machine?

Well, the obvious reason is that they don't want to pay out any more money than they have to. But many people also think to themselves, "I am going to be replacing this computer in about three years, so why get the latest and greatest model? I can save some money now, and just get a new one in three years." The stores reinforce this thinking by offering three-year warranties. This has a not-so-subtle message to the buyer, "In three years, this computer is going to fall apart."

So, all the Joe/Mary Jo average buyers out there start contributing to the vast landfill of old computers *even before they leave the store!* They are already planning on the end-of-life ceremony for their brand-new computer (or whatever product they buy).

This Is BAD THINKING!

The Math of Confidence

Look, if you buy a laptop for $600 you are still getting a great machine. It will do a LOT for you. You can take videos, watch movies, do paperwork, keep a calendar, etc. In fact, you can do almost anything the average person needs to do. Why would this laptop, made by a well-known computer company, only have a three-year lifespan?

Folks, you have to develop confidence in the stuff you buy. These are not disposable items. They are not going to become obsolete in a few years, just because the *advertising* says they are. These companies are trying to get you to think in a disposable mindset. They want you to *plan* on getting a new computer/camera/phone/whatever in just a few years.

That is how the retailers plan to stay in business. They want you to come into their store and shop for NEW as often as possible.

They are going to run Black Friday specials and sell add-ons that get you back in there, looking at upgraded laptops, etc. They want you to think like you are *leasing* these things, not buying them.

But, You Want Peace of Mind

On the other hand, there are the warranties. As Joe/Mary Jo buy the new iPhone for Joe Jr., they are thinking, "I know how rough he is on all his stuff. He is going to break that phone. I just know it."

Or, as they are buying that new laptop, they are thinking, "I just know this thing is going to fail. The hard drive will quit or I will have an electrical surge and everything will be fried. Why am I spending so much now on a machine that is going to fail?"

Or, as Joe and Mary Jo buy their car, they are thinking, "Wow, this is so complicated. The salesman said there are computers in there that might fail at any minute. The warranty only covers the drive train. By the way, what is a drive train? I just know I am going to have to spend thousands of dollars more on this car."

Look, it is natural to feel this way, because the retailers and the manufacturers, *want* you to feel this way. They want you to think, "*Something* is bound to go wrong, and I am going to have to pay for it. How am I going to afford it? Where will the money come from?"

The Gotcha Moment—Two Average Joes and a Dilemma

Joe and Mary Jo finally decided on a computer after working with the salesperson (another average Joe) at the Big Box store. Joe the buyer and Joe the salesman got very excited when talking about the power and speed of the new computer. Mary Jo got very excited when she learned how the new machine would help her get things done. *Everyone* was in agreement that the price was great and this was JUST the machine to do the work that the buying couple needed.

Joe the buyer took out his credit card, and then it happened…

Suddenly, Joe the salesman went from, "This is the very best technology on the market today and it is at such a wonderful price, imagine all the things you can do… " to, "This machine is going to fail within the first three years. You can expect a big puff of smoke and a loud whistle, just before all your data, photos and important documents are lost forever. In fact, it will probably happen very quickly—especially because of the dreaded "power surge" that is sure to be caused by the expansion of the sun… "

This is the "gotcha moment."

There is a huge shift in momentum. Suddenly, this wonderful product is no longer so wonderful. In fact, it is a wonder that it is still sitting there, without bursting into flames, as a power surge is certain to seek it out and destroy it.

How can the salesman do this? How can an "average Joe salesperson" go from, "I am pleased to sell you this incredible solution to all your tech problems," to "I have some terrible news. It is going to explode shortly," and still keep a straight face? How does an ordinary person make this transition, and then try to sell you a HUGELY

EXPENSIVE and OVER-PRICED warranty? And, how do they do it again and again, night after night, to other ordinary Joes?

The answer is simple: *training and incentives*.

You see folks, an ordinary person is probably NOT able to switch from the "this product is great" to the "this product is bound to fail" speech—unless they are *trained* to make this transition.

How does that average sales Joe turn from raving product fan into ranting product foe? You guessed it: *training*.

And, if training isn't enough (and it isn't), the Big Box retailers offer their employees *incentives* to do it. These incentives could be a commission or they could be, "If you don't do this, we will fire you and find someone who will do it." But, in any event, these incentives drive the behaviors that the Big Box retailers want from their "average Joes and Mary Jos." And those incentives really work, and in fact they DO drive them to make the switch from "fan to foe" and to sell warranties.

The Gotcha Moment is Really Just a Moment

When we call it the "gotcha moment," we really mean "moment." When is this magical moment? When do these two average people meet on the warranty battlefield? When is the exact moment of truth in this transaction?

The "gotcha moment" is when the average Joe, the buyer, takes out his credit card.

The next time you make a purchase that might need a warranty (which is for almost any product today, according to retailers) take note of the gotcha moment. It is like everyone in the back of the store is holding his/her breath. Watch the eyes of Joe the salesman. His eyes will narrow and focus. He is the perfectly trained sales machine!

He is looking for clues—for any telltale signs of weakness or resistance. He has an entire script at his disposal. He has been through training so that he has the perfect response for anything you, the average Joe the buyer, can throw at him.

He is ready, because the store has thought of this moment all day long. They thought of it all year long. They planned for this exact moment. They *dreamed* about it. And, their dreams are sweet! They are dreaming of this thing, this thought:

"We didn't make much money from the sale of that product, but wow, we can make a killing now!"

Profits—The *Full-Time* Pursuit of Retailers

The average buying Joe/Mary Jo is a part-timer. The selling Joe/Mary Jo is a full-time professional. And, the retailers who employ the selling Joe are *more* than full-time. The professionals who trained selling Joe are dead serious about what they do. They think about it all day, and they even have people who are supposed to think about it all night as well. They are working on that problem 24/7/366. (Yes, we said "366—these professionals even work on Leap Year!)

Here is a good story from Bill Quain that illustrates the difference:

Bill and Jeanne had two dogs named Abercrombie and Fitch (true!). Every day, Bill would go to work after Jeanne did and he would put the two dogs in the fenced backyard. Many times, he would come home from work and there would be Fitch, sitting in the FRONT yard. (Abercrombie never seemed to find a way out.)

Bill would pick up Fitch and carry her to the backyard, where he would spend a few minutes trying to figure out how she escaped. Sometimes he found it (and fixed it) and sometimes he did not. Even if he fixed it, however, Fitch would end up in the front yard a few days later, waiting for Bill to come home.

Bill asked Jeanne, "How is this dog outsmarting me? I have a Ph.D. and she is just a dog! (Note to husbands everywhere. Do NOT ask a question like this of your wife. It gives her too many smart-aleck answers!) After Jeanne *did* give Bill some smart-aleck replies, she gave him the answer that is a great lesson for any average buying Joe out there who is going up against any *selling Joes*.

Jeanne said, "Bill, you spend about ten minutes trying to figure out how Fitch is getting out of the backyard. She spends EVERY MINUTE of her day thinking about it. It doesn't matter how smart you are. You aren't a PROFESSIONAL at it like she is."

Folks, the same is true of the Big Box Retailers and you. It doesn't matter how smart you are or how much you think you are a smart shopper. They are spending every minute of every day thinking about how to get you to spend more money and they are training and rewarding their average Joe salespeople to take it from you.

You are not going to out-think the sales professionals who are selling you warranties.

You see folks, here is a BIG problem: warranties can be good. They do offer real benefits. But, if you are buying warranties, one at a time, at the gotcha moment—which is a moment of weakness—you are not getting a good deal. It is the exact moment when you should be saying, "I am NOT going to make an impulse buy right now. I am going to take my time and think about whether this makes sense monetarily. I am going to be smart about it."

But of course, the professionals are not going to give you the time to do the numbers. We call it the Gotcha Moment because, let's face it, they GOTCHA!

Turning Gotcha into Gotcha Covered

Folks, you are covered! Because you are a My Warranty Rewards Agent, you have protection already. You recognized that the products you buy CAN fail. But, you also realize that they can fail after the *three-year warranty has expired*! You have Matrix Protection and this eliminates the gotcha moment for you.

This gives you tremendous personal power. You can get the best deal from the Big Box store (or from an online retailer, or from a *small*

Big Box store, or wherever…) and then walk out of the store without ever thinking about the hard sales pitch from the selling Joe.

And, just as importantly, you can gain Peace of Mind for a lifetime by helping other people avoid the gotcha moment.

It doesn't get much better than that.

Chapter 7:
Behind the Scenes of the Warranty Biz

*"Formal education will make you a living.
Self education will make you a fortune."*

—Jim Rohn

According to Jay Tuerk, CEO of My Warranty Rewards, the warranty business has a fairly simple structure. As Jay puts it, "There are three major components of the industry: *the product, the Third Party Administrators, and the insurance company.*" In addition to these three components, we are going to add a fourth group to the discussion, the *repair centers* that get all your products working again.

As a My Warranty Rewards Independent Agent, you should be familiar with this underlying structure of the business. When you learn more about it, you will not only be amazed at just how simple this system is, but how powerful it can be. And, you will get an idea of just how fantastic the My Warranty Rewards opportunity is. You will discover several trade secrets that are actually substantial competitive advantages for My Warranty Rewards Agents.

The Product – In the warranty business, *warranties* (not surprisingly) are the products. The warranty is the set of terms and conditions set forth in the warranty documents. Warranty companies create warranty products, and sell them to customers. Now, don't get confused, the company that creates the warranty is NOT the Big Box Retailer or the Auto Dealership.

Trade Secret: the terms and conditions of almost all warranties are very similar. Most warranties promise to *repair, replace* or *reimburse* the customer for any covered terms.

Third Party Administrators (TPA) – when the average Joe/Mary Jo goes to a Big Box Retailer (BBR) to buy an item like a computer, the sales person presents them with a warranty product. These are NOT products created by the Big Box Retailer. The Big Box Retailer is in the business of doing two things: 1) selling products like computers, and 2) selling warranties. The BBR is NOT in the business of taking phone calls, repairing items, getting parts, handling complaints, etc. (these services, all the things that have to do with actually working with the warranty customers, are handled by a third party administrator). The TPA makes their money by selling warranties to BBR.

Trade Secret: There are only a handful of Third Party Administrators and they all sell the same product to the same Big Box Retailers and Auto Dealerships. How do Third Party Administrators compete for business if they are all selling the same basic product? They compete on price. (But up until now, this price competition did NOT result in lower prices for end users like you and me.)

The Insurance Company – Did you ever wonder where the money comes from to back up all the claims made on a warranty product? Before meeting Jay Tuerk, author Bill Quain thought it was just done by a group of investors. Instead, Jay showed Bill how warranties are heavily regulated and insurance companies back them all.

For example, have you bought life insurance? If you have, you will understand what an *actuarial table* is. The actuarial table is basically a forecast of how long you will live. The average life expectancies for both men and women are calculated using historical data. Insurance companies look at factors such as smoking and adjust your expected life range accordingly. These insurance companies then set a price for the insurance that is mathematically calculated to give them a predictable return.

Product insurance companies also estimate how long a product is expected to "live" and how often it might have to be repaired.

They also have a lot of facts about the average repair bill. (Did you know that the average *car* repair bill is $620 in the U.S.?) The insurance companies set the price they will charge the TPA for the warranty and the TPAs set a price they will charge the BBR.

Trade Secret: The insurance companies all use the same data to determine the cost of providing a product warranty. For example, the cost of a warranty for a Toshiba laptop is determined by standard industry data on Toshiba laptops. It isn't magical. It is *mathematical*.

The Repair Facilities – In the U.S. there are about 10,000 repair facilities that do warranty work on electronic items. (There are, of course, thousands of repair shops for automobiles as well.)

Trade Secret: Almost all the third party administrators send their electronic gadgets to one of these 10,000 facilities for repairs. Did you get that? **THEY ALL USE THE SAME REPAIR SHOPS.**

Summary

Few of the Big Box Retailers, and almost none of the car dealerships in the U.S., have their own warranties.

Most of them buy their warranties from Third Party Administrators. Almost all warranties are exactly the same. Take off the logo from the brochure, and they are all basically the same warranty. Insurance companies back up each of these warranty products.

How many insurance companies? We don't know, but there are not that many. And, almost all of the life expectancy and cost estimates are *exactly the same* from insurance company to insurance company. Finally, all warranty companies use the same repair centers to do repairs on the items under warranty.

How Does it Traditionally Work?

Let's say Big Box Retailer "A" is selling computers. They will be selling the same computers as Big Box Retailer "B" down the street. (Dell, Apple, Sony, Toshiba, etc.) Third party Administrator "C" creates a warranty product and gets it approved by Insurance Company "E." Third Party Administrator "D," ALSO creates a warranty product and they also get it backed by Insurance Company "E."

Both of the Third Party Administrators have call centers to answer customer calls, agreements with repair facilities, nicely printed brochures, computers and email addresses, etc. In other words, they are warranty companies. They sell warranties, and then they service them.

Third Party Administrators "C" and "D" are both trying to sell their products to Big Box Retailers "A" and "B." NEITHER of the Third Party Administrators is trying to sell warranties to end users. They have no way of reaching the end users for one thing, and for another, they have this great business going with the Big Box Retailers.

So, what is the differentiating factor between Third Party Administrators that would make a Big Box Retailer choose a Third Party Administrator over another? Certainly, *price* is a major factor. Remember, the Big Box Retailers are depending on the money they make by reselling these warranties.

Perhaps service or reliability is another factor, but let's face it, there isn't much difference between one insurance-company-backed warranty and another and there certainly isn't any difference among the repair facilities, because both Third Party Administrators are using the same ones!

In the end, the Big Box Retailer is going to choose the Third Party Administrator based on price, and on which TPA will get the fewest complaints from the end users. But, frankly, in most cases, it is a close call.

That is the Business

Isn't that simple? Can you see how this thing works and how My Warranty Rewards might be able to use Trade Secrets to *shake money out of this upside-down industry*?

In the next chapter, you will learn the BIG DIFFERENCES between My Warranty Rewards and the rest of the Warranty Industry, and how My Warranty Rewards will include YOU in the business of shaking money out of the industry—while giving the end users a much better deal!

Chapter 8:
Competition in the Peace of Mind Business

"Seek advice on risk from the wealthy who still take risks, not friends who dare nothing more than a football bet."

—J. Paul Getty

Advantage: My Warranty Reward

Competition is the heart and soul of business, but unfortunately, most people have never learned to compete. Schools don't teach it. Even most business people never learn it.

"Now wait," you are probably saying, "In school I was taught to compete against other students to get the highest honors. And in business, I am competing with my fellow workers to get the next raise or promotion."

Folks, that isn't what we are talking about here. As a My Warranty Rewards Independent Agent, you are in business for yourself and you are competing to win more business! You are competing to attract customers by giving them exactly what they want and you are going to give it to them better than anyone else.

Now, as an Independent My Warranty Rewards Agent, you are really in two businesses. You are in the Peace of Mind Business—but it has two levels. First, you are in the business of building business builders as you expand your My Warranty Rewards line and then you are in the Peace of Mind Warranty business as you sell warranties. In both cases you have competition. In both cases you can use your My Warranty Rewards Competitive Advantages to recruit other Agents and to recruit and retain warranty customers.

We will be talking about your My Warranty Rewards *Business of Building Business Builders* in the last section of this book. For now, let's talk about the competitive advantages that your Matrix Protection plan offers for the Warranty Peace of Mind Business.

But First, a Story to Help You Understand Competition

Two hikers, Frank and Joe, were out in the deep woods. As the two men came over a rise, they saw a huge grizzly bear, about a quarter of a mile away. The bear was *angry*. As the horrified hikers watched, the bear started running directly at them.

Joe calmly sat down and began to unpack running shoes from his backpack. He slipped off his hiking boots and began to lace up the running shoes.

Frank looked at him in amazement and said, "Joe, what are you doing? You can't outrun a bear."

Joe replied, "I don't have to outrun the *bear*. I just have to outrun YOU."

Folks, this is the story of competition. You don't have to be perfect in business (thank goodness!). You just have to be better than the competition. You need to be better, in some way, than the company or person that is trying to entice your customer.

> In business, you need to look
> for what we call sustainable
> competitive advantages.

Sustainable competitive advantages are the things that will mean the most to your clients and that will be advantageous for a long while. They are also called *sustainable* because it means that your company can keep offering them, because they fit into the profit goals of the company.

Your Sustainable Competitive Advantages

In order to understand how Matrix Protection's competitive advantages work, let's review a few things:

- Remember, right now, in the warranty market, there is a serious problem. Warranties are created for *retailers*, not *end users*.

- These products are *seriously* overpriced when the retailers sell them to the end user.

- Despite this, MILLIONS of end users buy them each year, and millions more *would* buy them if they were a better deal.

- Almost all warranties are exactly alike, because all those warranties are on the same products! (Best Buy sells a warranty on a Toshiba computer and so does Office Depot. It is the same laptop and the same warranty.)

- All the third party administrators use the same repair shops

- NOBODY is selling a low priced, *sensible* warranty directly to the end user.

The facts above open up what we call a "gap" in the marketplace. *Someone will fill that gap* because the demand and the profit potential are so high.

My Warranty Rewards has filled the gap by creating sustainable competitive advantages.

In the previous chapter, we discussed the four components of the Warranty Industry: 1) the product, 2) the Third Party Administrator, 3) the insurance company, and 4) the repair facilities.

My Warranty Rewards owns *two of the four* major components in the warranty business. They own the warranty products and they are also a Third Party Administrator. They don't need to own the repair facilities because these repair facilities serve ALL third party administrators. And My Warranty Rewards doesn't need to own the insurance company because the insurance companies all charge the same—because the insurance rates are all based on standard industry facts.

- Because they own the product (the warranties) and the Third Party Administrator, My Warranty Rewards can keep costs low and put more profit back into the hands of the Independent Agents.

- The Independent Agents are the commission-only sales force that reaches out to the end user. There are no profits being sucked up by Big Box Retailers. This means that My Warranty Rewards can lower their prices to the end users AND it still has plenty of money left over to give out to the Agents who build businesses.

My Warranty Rewards has a BIG competitive advantage. They got rid of the Big Box Retailers and created products that appeal to the end user with reasonable costs and profits. NO ONE ELSE is doing this.

And, guess what? Nobody else can easily duplicate this because no one else *owns* the two components (third party administrator and the warranty product) and has a Network Marketing Division that can reach end users without incurring massive costs!

Trade Secret—The only way to reach end users (consumers) is to either spend *millions and millions* of dollars on television advertising or go viral. Now, Social Media can help a company go viral. But, do you know what is even better? It is good, old-fashioned *networking*—the original "viral" marketing. The "average Joe/Mary Jo" is not going to set up a social media marketing campaign, but he/she can *talk* to a few friends and they will *talk* to a few friends… etc.

But, There is an Even BIGGER Sustainable Competitive Advantage

Okay, My Warranty Rewards is selling warranties through Network

Marketing—going viral by going face to face. This is good. In fact, it is great.

But there is something even better. It is something that taps into the very *heart* of what the end users want. It is the very best thing about this business because it is the very best thing for customers and business builders alike.

Are you ready for it? It is BIG, BIG, BIG!

With My Warranty Rewards, there is no Gotcha Moment.

You don't have to trap someone into buying a warranty at the very moment they just spent hundreds, or maybe even thousands of dollars on a product. You don't have to use strong-arm tactics or make up stories about lightning strikes, electricity surges, or other disasters.

You aren't trying to make a day's profit by selling warranties to your customers who just bought expensive stuff from you. You are selling Peace of Mind and you are selling it at any time—up to four years after they bought the product.

Folks, this is a *serious* sustainable competitive advantage.

You can show your customers how to *bundle* all of their stuff into one low-cost plan. You aren't asking them to take hundreds of dollars out of their wallets just to cover one thing. You are showing them how to get a warranty account that covers DOZENS of products. And those products do not have to be brand new. They do not even have to come from a Big Box Retailer. They can even be refurbished products in some cases.

Do you understand how BIG, BIG, BIG this is for you? It means that you are outrunning the competition on a HUGE issue for the customer. Heck, you might even be outrunning the BEAR!

You are Selling Peace of Mind, Because You are Selling Control

Look, we talked about some of the things that people hate about buying warranties. They know they are being ripped off. They don't like laying out a ton of money—right after buying something. They don't like the pressure. They don't want to be rushed. They hate trying to keep track of all the warranties. They know that a three-year warranty is going to run out just before the product dies. They know and hate all these things.

YOU have the solution.

YOU have control over a situation that has been running amuck for many years, and YOU are going to give that control directly to the people who are buying the warranties just so they could have control in their lives.

Control = Peace of Mind

This is SERIOUS Stuff

Folks, you have something BIG on your plate right now. You are part of a movement that is going to make *millions* of people happier. You are going to give people more control over their lives and they are going to reward you. My Warranty Rewards is going to reward you. (Did you think they named it My Warranty *Rewards* by accident?)

You are finally at the right place at the right time. You have a wonderful product, with exceptional benefits. It is just what MILLIONS of people want. This is YOUR time.

So, What do You Have to DO?

A few pages ago, we said that selling directly to end-users requires either MILLIONS of dollars (think television infomercials) or it takes some sort of viral marketing. TV advertising is expensive. It has to be repeated again and again.

Viral marketing can keep a steady stream of messages going out at all times, and it is very cost effective. With TV advertising, you spend MILLIONS *before* you make even hundreds of dollars. With viral network marketing, you spend just *thousands* of dollars before the product sells millions, and then you *distribute the millions* among the people who made the sales.

And guess what? The networkers, the engines of the viral marketing effort, spend almost NOTHING before they begin making money.

EVERYONE wins—the company, the customers, and the MARKETERS.

In the third section of this book, we are going to show you how to become a low-cost, but very high-result viral network marketer. You don't need Twitter or Facebook. There is no hocus-pocus marketing. You simply have to tell the story. You are looking for people who are also looking.

What are they looking for?

Peace of Mind!

Some people want just a little Peace of Mind through product warranties. You can take care of them.

Some people only want a little Peace of Mind through a small income. You can take care of them.

But, some people are looking for BIG TIME Peace of Mind. They want to get rid of stress, take vacations with family and friends, grow strong relationships, and enjoy recognition from other people who have broken out of the bonds that hold the average Joes in virtual economic slavery to the dreams and ambitions of other men and women.

Folks, you want them all! Are you ready? Keep reading!

𝔓eace of 𝔐ind

Business Times

Yoni Ashurov

Yoni Ashurov believes in stripping business down to the basics. Without inventory, store displays and products to ship, his business minimizes expenses and maximizes profits, a model that benefits those who sell and those who buy.

It's a total win-win, as he sees it, and it's one of the reasons My Warranty Rewards has been able to thoroughly disrupt the conventional warranty world in such a short amount of time.

As Co-Founder and President of My Warranty Rewards, Ashurov, in 2013, created a distribution platform for a warranty plan that requires no manufacturing facilities, no costly inventory, and no transportation system. Independent Agents digitally sell Matrix Protection, a warranty plan that covers electronics products for $29.97 a month, without ever clocking in at the main office. In other words, a giant departure from the way the $50 billion Warranty Industry has traditionally done business.

"This really opened my eyes to the sheer power of network marketing as a distribution force," Ashurov said. "Network marketing is the last bastion of alternative distribution out there."

In building a business, Ashurov adheres to the following five key tenets, which he likens to spokes on a wheel:

1. Unique product. Not necessarily exclusive, but also not readily available from multiple vendors in multiple locations. It is "critical" that the product have wide appeal to a wide audience, have no geographical boundaries, and create demand for repeat purchases.

"It has to be innovative," Ashurov said, "something people can get excited about."

2. Proper compensation. Getting to the break-even point should happen within 30 days and earning the $500 extra the average person is looking to make monthly (residual income) should happen quickly, too. "The average bankruptcy happens to people who are $5,000 short in a year," Ashurov said. "That extra $500 a month would stave off many bankruptcies." But MWR's Comp Plan isn't just for breaking even. My Warranty Rewards also offers a 25% check match to agents who bring others into the business. As Yoni puts it, "We have a plan for anyone, no matter how large their dreams are."

3. Positive culture. A support system for those who need guidance, until they establish confidence in the business, is essential to success.

"If everybody was a born entrepreneur, they wouldn't need the yellow brick road to follow," Ashurov said. "The biggest battle is mental and

(Continued)

emotional. The reason why people quit is they don't have support."

He views himself (and other MWR leaders) as a guide for the Agents. "We work directly with any Agent who requires direction. Working like this, we build a strong foundation based on integrity." He also believes in making himself available to Agents.

"It's important for people to get to meet us and know us," he said.

4. Duplicable system. Simple and easy instructions for all facets of the business, including training and core service values. Knowing what steps to follow sequentially eliminates guesswork and reduces mistakes.

"Confidence is something that is built, step-by-step at MWR. It is part of our culture."

5. Infrastructure and scalability. Appropriate financial and human resources are required to successfully handle explosive growth. Matrix Protection already manages more than 600,000 warranties, so the addition of hundreds of thousands more isn't going to overwhelm the company.

"I can't say that one is more important than another," Ashurov said of the five tenets. "If you fail at any one of them, you're not going to be successful. You must excel at all of them!"

A former real estate broker in Panama who managed 40 in-house agents, Ashurov learned long ago how to motivate people. Providing them with a proven business structure is a necessary professional consideration. But nurturing personal relationships matters to him, too.

"I listen when people come to me," he said. "How you treat other people is important. You need to show respect, fairness and honesty. My whole business career, I have been around agents, so I truly understand their value to the business world."

Life, he said, is more than a transaction.

"If we build a great foundation and have the right motives, the Agent succeeds and the customer is happy," Ashurov said. "It's not rocket science."

While My Warranty Rewards is first to market with a radically different approach to selling warranties, the company is looking to "continually improve," Ashurov said, and sustain its forward momentum.

"A lot of companies are victims of complacency," he said. "We're never comfortable with the status quo."

Chapter 9:
S.M.I.L.E.S: The Peace of Mind Hierarchy

"When you've seen beyond yourself, then you may find peace of mind is waiting there."

—George Harrison

Human beings are funny people. They all go through the same set of feelings when it comes to solving their problems. You can't get them to think about the big picture when they are facing imminent danger or need.

Here is a good example:

A man was stranded on a desert island without food or water. After a few days, he was in a very bad way. He was thirsty and hungry, and had lost hope of being rescued.

He had done all the things that people who are stranded on a desert island do. He wrote "HELP" in the sand, tried to signal planes with tin foil, and built shelter.

On the fifth day, just as he was about to give up entirely, a plane started circling his island. He ran to the tin foil and began reflecting the sun into the plane's cockpit so the pilots couldn't miss it.

It turned out that the plane was a seaplane, and it landed just off the island. A beautiful woman, a trained rescue specialist, sprang into a rubber raft and began to paddle to the beach. As she reached the man, she smiled and said, "I have food and water for you. We are going to fly you to safety. Do you want water first, food first, or do you want to just get into the raft with me and let me take care of you while the pilots fly you home?"

Well, the man knew his priorities. He was too weak to get into the raft. He couldn't swallow any food. He just wanted—and needed—water. "Water," he rasped. "Water is all I need right now."

The beautiful woman lifted a canteen of cool water to the man's lips. As he began to drink the life-saving liquid, she suddenly grabbed his throat and began to squeeze. She wouldn't let go, and the man had to drop the bottle of water and slap her hand hard, just so he could breathe…

What is the purpose of this story? Why are we telling it in this book?

If you intend to solve your Peace of Mind problems, you are going to have to learn about people's motivations. In general, people will always fill their most urgent needs first. When the man was just *thirsty*, getting water was his most urgent need. But, as soon as he was deprived of *air*, that became his top priority. When he started to lose his oxygen, he reacted forcefully. It was his most urgent need.

Oh, and one more thing…

Were you wondering what we were going to tell you about the fact that a beautiful woman was the one who rescued the man? Were you thinking, "What does her beauty have to do with this story?" Here is the answer and it is a *beautiful* thing for anyone who wants to motivate others. It is a *beautiful* thing because we sometimes become fearful that we are not the right messengers to motivate others.

TAKE NOTE: If you were thinking, "It wouldn't have mattered to that man if a beautiful woman or an ugly man was bringing water to the man on the island." He didn't care who helped him out. He was so consumed with the fact that he desperately needed *relief* from his pain that he would have accepted water from his worst enemy.

Why is this an important message for you?

If you are going to work with other people, never worry about what they think of you. In fact, if the pain is great enough, YOU become inconsequential.

YOU aren't even in their minds at all. If they are truly in need of relief, *stopping the pain* is all that is important.

Are They Thirsty, or Do They Need Air?

Earlier in the book, we showed our 100 comments about Peace of Mind Disrupters. These comments were taken from a sample of friends. None of the people we spoke with were *poor*. None of them were on the brink of disaster. All of them had jobs, or were successfully self-employed. Yet, the vast majority of the comments we received were economic in nature. *All of the people* who commented were concerned, to some degree, about financial issues.

Yes, some of them also had health, family and technology issues. And, a few had self-worth worries that disrupted their Peace of Mind, but financial stuff was the big one.

Why is that? Well, these people had all just come through a very tough recession. Many of them were not living as well, or as securely, as they had been before the recession. It was on their minds a great deal of the time. It was their water and not their food. And, they were all afraid that a new setback would set them to *choking and gasping for air* again.

Now, one of the people who talked to us about the Peace of Mind Disrupters is a very successful person. He built massive businesses over the last fifteen years and he is very wealthy. More importantly, his wealth keeps growing every month, no matter if he works on it or not. This man had a completely different set of disrupters. In fact, he didn't talk to us about disrupters at all. Instead, he told us about the things that *do* bring him Peace of Mind, not the things that disrupt it.

What did he say? Here is a short list of his top Peace of Mind issues:

1. Being a good dad and husband and a good provider for his family

2. Leading by example

3. Giving back to an industry that has been so good to him

4. Helping others reach their dreams and goals

5. Doing something no one else has accomplished

Let's take a look at his views on Peace of Mind. Certainly, the first issues "good dad, husband, provider…" is something that almost everyone is concentrating on. But, look at some of the others, especially "do something no one else has done…" This is a different kind of issue, isn't it?

The man who sent us these comments has already taken care of his financial worries. Because of that, he can concentrate on higher-level ideals. And, this brings up an important concept. When you are working with people to help them find Peace of Mind, be sure to work with them on the level where they are now!

Maslow's Hierarchy of Needs

In 1943, a man named Abraham Maslow came up with his Hierarchy of Needs. According to Maslow, everyone tends to "move up the ladder" as they fulfill basic needs and as they improve their conditions, they tend to concentrate on different needs—mainly those of self-worth. Maslow's Hierarchy is taught in almost every business school and to every psychology student.

Here is a picture of Maslow's Hierarchy:

Notice how the basic needs are things like water, air, etc. At the top, Maslow says that men and women are looking for self-actualization (esteem, fulfillment, accomplishment, etc.). According to his theory, people must get the basics first and then they are motivated by higher goals.

This makes sense. Just like the man on the island at the beginning of this chapter, people will always focus on the most pressing, most basic need first, and then they can be motivated to aim higher.

S.M.I.L.E.S: A More Modern Maslow

In 1996, Bill Quain was on his way to deliver a presentation to a group of independent business people in Florida. Bill was thinking about Maslow and how it applied to modern business building. Bill is a big believer that, "In order to get what you want, you have to help others get what *they* want." But, Bill also knew that people were all in a unique place when they first see a business opportunity. And, he wanted to find some way to demonstrate this to the people in his audience. That is when he came up with his ideas for S.M.I.L.E.S.

These letters stand for:

S. – <u>Survival</u>—No one is going to think about getting a new boat if they can't pay the rent. If you, or one of your business associates is in the Survival stage, you need to concentrate on the basics. As the saying goes, "You want to have as much money as you have month." In other words, the first priority is to be able to pay the bills.

M. – <u>Material</u>—It is okay to *want* things. It really is. You don't need to be materialistic. You just have to want things in a real and meaningful way. That is why so many successful people put pictures of the things they want on their refrigerator. It is a motivator. It is okay! If you find people at this stage, show them how to get the things they want. It is very motivating.

I. – <u>Income</u>—Some people say, "If I could just make _____ dollars more per month, it would be fantastic. It would take all the pressure off me." This is an excellent Peace of Mind stage, because the extra money will absolutely help to create more Peace of Mind. But, these people may run into two problems. First, if they make more money, but start buying more things on credit, they are putting themselves into a vicious cycle. Second, if the money is not *residual*, meaning it continues to come in whether they are working or not, it may mean working too many hours to enjoy the money! However, Income *can be* a fantastic motivator.

L. – <u>Lifestyle</u>—Now we are talking! Lifestyle is defined as "Money, and the time to spend it." Lifestyle is a fantastic dream stage. When you are working with someone, ask them, "What would you do if time and money were not a problem?" We have asked this question of so many people. Do you know what the first answer is (about 90% of the time)? Most people say, "I would travel." By the way, a great follow-up question is, "Okay, where is the first place you would go and how long would you stay?" Can you see how motivating this would be?

E. – <u>Expressive</u>—Bill often asks people, "If time and money were not a problem (meaning that you have enough of both of them), how would you express yourself?" Now THIS is motivating—but only if you are at least out of the survival stage! One man told Bill, "I love the arts, but I am not talented. I can't play an instrument, but for me, becoming a major sponsor of the arts, particularly the opera, would be fantastic." Another man, a childhood friend of Bill's, said, "I would like to help mentally challenged children. That would be a great satisfaction to me." (This man was a truck driver and it floored Bill when his friend told him this.)

S. – <u>Spiritual</u>—How would you best serve God if you were able to do it? What kind of person would you become as you took care of all the other cares and issues that clutter your life? For many people, the best way to serve God is to serve your fellow man. And, the first thing you need to do in order to effectively serve others is to take care of all the problems in your own life.

Putting the S.M.I.L.E.S. Back into the American Dream

At this point in the book, you know something that most people never figure out. You know where you are in the Peace of Mind journey. You have completed an 80/20 analysis of your Peace of Mind Disrupters and you know where you stand in the Hierarchy of Needs.

Are you most concerned about financial issues or health issues? If so, you might be on some of the lower stages of the hierarchy. However, are you beginning to think to yourself, "Well, I am not in bad shape financially, but I now need more time in my life?" If so, maybe you are peeking into one of the higher stages.

Now look folks, this doesn't mean that you can't get excited about lifestyle or spiritual dreams if you are short on cash. It just means that you need to *balance* those things. If you are worried about money (and the vast majority of people are) then you have to make money your top priority. After all, this is why you did the 80/20 analysis in the first place. But, it doesn't hurt to start thinking about some of the other goodies in life as well. We want you to think BIG, because we are going to show you how to do BIG things. The title of this book is Peace of Mind, not Pay Your Phone Bill, right?

Motivating Others

If you are working with other people, it is critical that you address their basic needs first.

But, it is also critical that you expose them to bigger dreams. Get them thinking beyond their current circumstances. This will give you tremendous power. It will help you build a big business by making you an expert at helping others build their businesses.

Remember, it Isn't About You

Think back to the story at the beginning of this chapter. Do you remember our message about the beautiful woman who brought the man his water and food? The man didn't think to himself, "Okay, I will take this water, but only because the woman is beautiful." No, he was just thinking, "I am so thirsty. Where is the water?"

Let us tell you one thing with certainty right now. At this stage, knowing what you know about Peace of Mind and disrupters, and knowing what you know about human pain caused by an unfilled need, you have tremendous power. You don't have power *over* people. You have power *with* people. You have the power to change lives, starting with your own life. You have the power to help yourself and others gain Peace of Mind.

Now, take your power and grow!

Chapter 10:

Network Marketing: Own Your Business and Own Your Life

"If you want to work the rest of your life, that's your business. If you don't want to work the rest of your life, that's MY business."

—Tim Rose, network marketer

In the United States we have become a nation of renters, not owners. Look at the things you *think* you own—your home, your car, your technology and even your most precious commodity, your TIME. Do you realize that the average American does not own *any* of these things?

Instead, we are all paying off mortgages, car loans, college loans and credit cards. You don't even own your access to information. Instead, we pay a monthly fee to the cable company and the phone company for our Internet and television privileges.

The average American family has over $7,000 in credit card debt that they will NEVER pay off because they are *renting* that money and paying interest every month.

You don't even own your time anymore, do you? After all, don't you go to work every day and spend hour after hour working on someone else's dream? You do one hour of work and they give you one hour of pay. And most people would say, "Well, that proves it. I own my time because I am selling it to my boss. If I didn't own my time, how could I sell it?"

But in reality, your time is worthless *except for the fact that someone else created a business for you to work in*! Think about it. What happens to the value of your time if you get fired or laid off? How much is it worth then?

The American Dream—According to the Politicians

We watch the politicians argue on television. They are all saying things like:

"More Americans need to be able to afford a nice home," and "We need more good-paying jobs for Americans."

Yes, the American Dream has become closely related to those two things. But, how many people actually *love* the work they do and feel that it is meaningful and that they are well paid?

And how many Americans actually own their homes? We don't know and it really doesn't matter, because we are willing to bet that almost every one of our readers has a mortgage. We are willing to bet that almost NONE of our readers actually own his/her home outright.

Yet, the politicians insist that a person owns their home if that person has some kind of mortgage on it. Our politicians insist that home ownership is measured by the number of people who have a mortgage, not by the number of people who have a home with NO mortgage!

Do you remember 2008? What was one of the biggest causes of the last recession? What brought down the whole house of cards? It was the huge number of mortgages that were sold to unqualified buyers and then re-packaged and sold to unqualified investors!

The American Dream Myth Almost Killed the American Dream—*Permanently*

Look, we aren't going to get too bogged down in this discussion, but it is definitely worth the time to remember what happened. Ironically, it was the American Dream MYTH that almost wrecked our economy for good.

Here is a brief history:

1. Housing prices were rising.

2. Mortgage brokers were selling homes to people who could not afford them.

3. People signed loans that they did not understand.

4. Appraisers were telling banks that the houses were worth more than the actual worth.

5. Banks (full of smart people) lent money to anyone who asked for it.

6. It turned out that the banks actually were full of smart people, because they sold the loans to investment banks.

7. The investment banks were the smartest of all, because they sold the bad loans to investors and then took out insurance to bet against their investment customers.

8. The investors, who we all *thought* were smart enough to understand what they were buying, instead of just throwing investment money at anything that the brokers said was good, lost billions of dollars.

What was the result of all this? Well, ordinary investors went broke. Homeowners (who didn't really own a home—just a mortgage) lost their homes or, in many cases, ended up paying more for the house than it was worth.

And, all of this was based on the American dream of home ownership. But you see, it wasn't home ownership—it was *mortgage* ownership. And what is a mortgage? It is essentially a renter's agreement between the bank (that actually owns the house) and a tenant (the person who thinks he/she owns the house).

Let's face it; you really don't own much in your life, do you?

You don't own your home, your car, and your stuff that is still being paid off on your credit cards, or even your time. You are broke and you are renting! Worse, you are locked into mortgages, credit card loans, car loans and your boss's factory or office. You are a virtual slave, with little property and not much chance of ever owning anything.

Okay, let's lighten it up...

Let us cap off this really stressful part of the book with a little joke that makes the point—but will get you laughing as well.

A very successful businessman had a favorite uncle. Unfortunately, the uncle died suddenly and the businessman was on an extended trip abroad. The businessman called the funeral director and said, "This man was my favorite uncle and I can't even be there for the funeral. So, I want you to give him the biggest, most impressive send-off that money can buy. Do it up right and send me the bill. It is the least I can do for my favorite uncle."

The funeral was, by all accounts, a grand affair. The businessman heard all about it from the other relatives, who all said that the uncle would have loved it. Thirty days later, the funeral director sent the businessman a bill for $50,295.

"This is a lot of money," thought the nephew, "but I did tell them to do it right." He paid the bill.

Thirty days later, the businessman got another bill for $295. He paid it. One month after that, he got another bill for $295. He paid it as well. But, when he got yet another bill for $295 for the *third* month in a row, he called the funeral director to ask what was going on.

"Well," said the funeral director, "you said you wanted a great send off, didn't you?"

"I did," said the nephew.

"And you wanted your uncle to look great, didn't you?"

"I did," said the man.

"Well, it was a great funeral and he looked just fine. In fact, we rented him a tuxedo so he would look even better."

Do you see where this is going? We do the same things in our lives, don't we? We put ourselves into endless rental situations that we know will never pay off: mortgages, credit card balances, auto loans.

And worst of all, we rent space at work, just so we can be paid less than we are worth—for a working lifetime.

But Wait—the Dream is Still Alive!

Folks, you can end this vicious cycle at any time. All you have to do is to start owning your life again. All you have to do is to say, "Enough is enough. I am going to stop this craziness. I am going to own my life, not just rent it."

How do you own your life again? It is easy.
You just need to own your own business,
and then use the profits you generate
to buy back your life.

Your job is never going to pay off all those debts. It is not going to do it for two reasons. First, your boss is never going to pay you enough to live as a free man or woman—a person who has no debt, but who also has everything that he/she wants out of life. Second, in order to make enough money to pay off all the things you need in life, you have to keep working, hour-after-hour and year-after-year, for the rest of your life. You can never stop working! You can never take the time off to enjoy your life because the minute you stop working, you stop getting paid!

No, in order to have enough money—and the time to enjoy it—you must be the owner of your business. And, you must have the kind of business that produces income for you every minute of every day—whether you work or not.

Do you know of any kind of business that will do this for you? Well, you know there is, or you would not still be reading this book. You know what kind of business this is. It is network marketing.

Low-Risk Business Ownership

Earlier in this book, we used the phrase, "gaining peace of mind without losing it." By this we meant that most people encounter too much risk when they take on a business. If you wanted to build a McDonald's franchise, do you realize that you would need a million dollars before the McDonald's corporation would even consider your application for a location? Why? Because they want to make sure you can get through the incredible start-up costs while you grow your business. You have to build a site, hire and pay employees, advertise, purchase food and pay taxes.

But, what if there was a business—a real business—that cost you almost nothing to start? And, what if that business had almost no ongoing costs? But, what if that same business had extremely high payouts and those payouts would continue as long as the business you built continued?

This is the beauty of network marketing. It is, in fact, the American dream business. You have ownership with no debt. You have access to all the products, information, assistance and training you will ever need. You have almost no overhead.

You are the boss. You are in control. You get the rewards for your work—not someone who just happens to be the boss's nephew!

But, here is the best news for people who are sick and tired of losing money, paying off debt, and working harder and harder for less and less:

You can pay for your business by just changing a few of your habits.

Your entire investment is less than the price of a few meals in a restaurant. All you need to do is to make just a few changes in your life choices and you can have the keys to your own business.

What are you doing right now that will cost you more than the investment cost in your business? Consider these choices:

- You are going to restaurants too often. Have a few meals with your family each month instead.

- You are throwing out perfectly good technology—just to get a newer model that really doesn't give you anything more than your old model.

- You are trading in a perfectly good car—just because you want a newer one.

Folks, if you just stopped doing these three things you could afford a business that would set you free. You already have the money you need to get this thing going and keep it going. You are just spending it on stuff that will keep you a slave to a boss for the rest of your life.

We know you can't change your mortgage payment right now. And, we know you can't get out of your car lease, your phone plan and those other things that run up the bill every month. We know that.

But, we also know that you need to make some changes and we think you know that as well. So, why not make some smart changes that will set you free instead of dumb choices that will keep you enslaved?

The Risk is Long-Term, not Short-Term

When most people look at a business opportunity like network marketing, they think, "I don't want to lay out a few hundred dollars right now. That is too much money." Yet, those same people will lock themselves into long-term debt and never-ending agreements! For those people, we have a two-word bit of advice that you will see in other parts of this book. It is:

"Stop it!"

Don't throw away your future, just because you are afraid to make a few changes. Pay yourself for your network marketing business by staying at home for a few meals per month or by packing your lunch instead of going out to eat.

Why are you spending $10 for a fancy coffee and a pastry for breakfast when your entire life is mortgaged to a bank and to a boss?

We just don't understand why Americans will trade their real American dream for a fatty American diet!

In the next few chapters, you are going to learn why the My Warranty Rewards network marketing business can be your ticket to the American dream—without losing your peace of mind—or your hard-earned money.

When Owning is Ordinary and Achievement is Average

There used to be a television show called "Lifestyles of the Rich and Famous." Network marketers aren't looking for extraordinary people like the "rich and famous." Networkers want the average Joe and Mary Jo. Yet, they want to help those average people achieve an extraordinary lifestyle. But, here is the interesting thing: networkers want so many people to enjoy an above average lifestyle that it actually becomes *average* to live that way.

Want to be part of the fun? Let's change the averages, shall we?

Chapter 11:
Activate Your Agency Equity

"The entrepreneur always searches for change, responds to it, and exploits it as an opportunity."

—Peter Drucker

As a My Warranty Rewards *Agent*, you have tremendous equity. You can leverage that equity to make money. But, in order to maximize your money-making potential, you need to understand the unique relationship between an Agent and the parent company. When you do, you will be amazed at just how much power your position gives you. You have the power to change your life and the lives of other Agents you bring to the business.

What is an Agent?

Most of us are familiar with two types of Agents—Insurance Agents and Real Estate Agents. These Agents *represent* buyers and sellers. They bring the buyer and seller together. Agents do not own the product. They do not invest money into the transaction. Instead, their job is simply to *create* the transaction and to help both parties (seller and buyer) understand the benefits that they will receive.

Sound a bit confusing? No problem. Let's look at a Real Estate transaction to see how this works.

Joe is a Real Estate *Agent*. He works at a Real Estate *Agency*. Joe is not an employee of the Real Estate Agency. Instead, he is a sort of independent contractor. Joe has a desk at the Agency and he is able to use the Agency's name, files, secretarial staff, etc.

Mary Jo wants to sell her home and she asks Joe to sell it for her. Joe agrees and tells Mary Jo that he will expect a 6% commission for listing the house on the Multiple Listing service, showing it to potential buyers, taking care of the settlement when the house sells, and keeping Mary Jo up-to-date on what is happening in the market. Mary Jo agrees, because she doesn't want to take the time to go out and find buyers for her house. She is thrilled that Joe will do that work for her.

Joe's MAIN job is to find buyers. He is the one who will go to his contact list, talk to other agents, place signs on the lawn, etc. Joe is bringing great *value* to Mary Jo. Mary Jo *wants* someone like him to do the work.

But, Joe is not Alone.

If Joe did everything on his own, it would be very costly. He would have to hire lawyers to look over all his contracts and proposals. He would need to spend LOTS of money to join the Multiple Listing Service System that lists houses for other Real Estate Agents to see. He would have to hire secretaries and receptionists to handle the phones and the customers who walk into the door.

In addition, Joe would have to develop websites with background information for online shoppers. This also requires someone to take photos of the home and post them online. Finally, when the home sells, Joe would need to find an office where the buyer and the seller could come together to sign the contracts, and Joe would need to make arrangements with local banks to handle all the money, and attorneys to check over all the signatures, clauses, etc.

This would all be very expensive and very time-consuming. Frankly, Joe doesn't want to do all that because it would take away from the time he puts into actually bringing buyers and sellers together. You see folks, bringing together the buyer and seller is the ONLY place where Joe can make money. He doesn't make money from any of the other things that have to happen so a home will sell.

So, Joe becomes an Independent Agent at an *Agency*. The Agency does all the "grunt" work for Joe. The Agency is happy to do it because they have lots of Joes working with them. The Agency is glad to do all the background work because it makes it easier for all the selling-Joes out there to create transactions. Joe is not alone because he is an Agent and his Agency supports him. The Agency makes it easy for Joe to sell.

You are a My Warranty Rewards Agent

You are an Agent. Your job is simple. You are going to use your contacts and your network, to tell the Matrix Protection story. You *represent* the product. Like Joe, you are simply there to create transactions and to help both customers and other Agents understand the benefits of My Warranty Rewards and Matrix Protection.

You are not alone. You do not have to do all the "grunt" work, nor hire attorneys, nor do the accounting. You do not have to create products, test them, monitor them, make payouts, hire support staff, etc. You are free to do the one thing that My Warranty Rewards wants you to do. More importantly, you are free to do the one thing you want to do in this business—make money! My Warranty Rewards does not want you to get bogged down in the agonizing details of the business. You are an AGENT!

This Gives You Equity

The minute you make the modest investment of a couple of hundred dollars, you gain incredible equity. You become an Agent IMMEDIATELY after signing up with My Warranty Rewards. Think about it. One minute, you are NOT an Agent, and the next minute, YOU HAVE IT ALL! And, once you have it all, you can use it to start making money!

What do you receive for your investment? Here is just a short list:

1. A personalized, customized website, with promotional videos to attract customers and new Agents.

2. A full Back Office that tracks every one of your customers and downline.

3. The ability to sell the finest, most reasonably priced warranty on the market. It is the ONLY *lifetime* warranty currently available.

4. Complete legal and administrative support. My Warranty Rewards has already done all the heavy lifting. The product is ready to go. It is approved.

5. Top-of-the-line education and training. You get the benefit of *experience* as proven leaders show you exactly what to do to make money.

6. All the branding, positioning and image-building of a world-class product and leadership.

7. Most importantly, you get the full attention of experts who will join you in sales calls, work with your downline, answer questions from your customers, etc.

You OWN This Stuff

YOU own it because you own your Agency. You get all of the things listed above and MORE—simply by making a commitment of about two hundred dollars. What is the *value* of the new stuff you own? What is the *value* of legal support, a world-class product, your website, your Back Office, the expertise of the leaders who will make phone calls with you, the training and education you receive, and all the other stuff that makes this arrangement so attractive?

We are about to tell you what the exact value of all this stuff is. It is worth absolutely NOTHING if you don't use it to make money. If you make the incredibly low investment of a couple of hundred dollars and do NOTHING about it, then your investment is worth NOTHING and all that equity is worth NOTHING.

On the other hand, if you do SOMETHING you will be amazed at how quickly the value grows. You don't have to be perfect. You just have to get started!

The Big Secret of Agency Equity

In order to earn the equity that is waiting, you have to *activate* that equity.

You have to do something in order for it to be of any value at all. Did you ever buy some computer software or an app for your phone? You have to *activate* that software in order for it to be of value. If you just download it, and never use it, it has no value. Worse yet, it is simply taking up space on your screen!

When you *activate* your equity, you open the door to expertise and assistance. Your upline sponsors are going to do everything they can to help you. My Warranty Rewards has experts who will actually get on the phone with your prospects. You do not have to be a Warranty expert in order to activate your equity. My Warranty Rewards has all the experts you need.

No, in order to activate your equity, all you have to do is what MWR wanted you to do all along. It is the thing they are paying you to do. It is the thing that YOU SHOULD WANT to do if you want to make money.

All you have to do to activate your equity is to follow the MWR Success System... sharing this innovative service. That's it. But, unless you do this one thing, you will never be successful as an MWR Agent.

How do I Maximize My Rewards for Sharing?

The simple answer is this: "Leverage." As an MWR Agent you want to focus your attention on making money by sharing the opportunity and product. But, while both of these activities will make you money, only one will actually *leverage* your equity. So, which one is it? Which of the two "sharing activities" activates *"leveraged equity" and therefore, activates the BIG money*?

If you answered, "Sharing the opportunity," then you are correct.

Remember, MWR wants you to help build the business FAST. And they are going to put their biggest rewards into the sharing activities that help to do just that—build fast. Sharing the *opportunity* is the key to fast growth, explosive growth—the kind of awesome growth that will develop long-term financial success. It is the kind of growth that generates Peace of Mind.

Be in the Business of Building Business Builders

Become an Agent of Change, and an Agent of Growth, not just a product Agent.

If you want to activate the highest-paying equity, concentrate on building other Agents.

This activates *leverage* because those Agents are also activating their equity. Folks, as we always say, "This isn't rocket science." It is just a matter of figuring out why MWR is so interested in what you have to offer. They don't want your money, they just want your actions, and they are going to reward you in such a way that the actions they really want—building business builders—is what you will focus on.

MWR is going to handle *everything* else. They are going to take care of all the grunt work for you. You are free to build your business by doing ONLY the things that will bring you money and you are free to pursue the things that will bring you the most money for the least amount of effort.

Why? It is simple. MWR wants to go viral and you are going to help them do that.

You are at the right place, at the right time. Now, take Ray Kroc's advice and do something about it. Activate your equity and leverage your business by building business builders.

How much will your Agency Equity be worth if you *activate* it by *activating* yourself? The value could be priceless! You see, if you *activate* that equity, you can start making some money right away. You can then start making some more money. Pretty soon, you will unlock the power of RESIDUAL INCOME by helping OTHER AGENTS get activated. At that point, you can start changing your world.

Imagine the personal feeling of satisfaction at regaining control over your financial destiny. Imagine the feeling you will get when your family starts to see you as the great example you will become.

Your Equity is worth exactly what you put into it. It isn't the $200 investment that unlocks the equity. It is the *energy* that you put into the program *that creates the value*.

We Told You that My Warranty Rewards Wants What You Have

Earlier in this book we told you that My Warranty Rewards was looking specifically for you. They didn't want your money. They wanted your actions.

Chapter 12:
Leverage or Be Leveraged— The Business Rule for ALL Businesses

"It is better to own half a watermelon than a whole grape."

—Bill Quain

It was another of those outstanding moments for an author. We were listening to a phone call from Yoni Ashorav, President of My Warranty Rewards. Yoni is soft-spoken and you have to listen carefully to what he says because he has some great thoughts, excellent perspectives, and mind-blowing pronouncements. But, they all come in this quiet voice that might fool you if you are not careful.

So, we were listening and we were glad we were!

Ironically, Yoni started off his talk with a discussion of *leverage*, and we were just at this very point in writing the book. We had already decided that this key chapter would be about leverage and here was Yoni, in his quiet, calm voice, laying out the most incredible explanation of this topic we ever heard. So, here is a recap of his presentation and some add-ons from us.

"You are Either Leveraging or Being Leveraged"

Bam! Beautiful stuff! And you know what? It is so true!

In this business, you either leverage your equity and assets, and turn them into something more, or you are the one who is leveraged.

- If you are being leveraged, you are part of someone else's dream.
- If you are applying leverage, you are taking something you own and making it into a powerful, income generating machine.

There is really no middle ground here. If you are a worker, trading your time for dollars, someone else is leveraging you. If you are a business owner, a builder, you are taking your equity and creating more value—lots and lots of value.

Now look, we wanted to start this chapter off with a powerful set of statements and we chose Yoni's words to do it. But we realize that many people really don't understand what leverage is. They have heard of the term, but the average Joe or Mary Jo just doesn't get it because no one ever taught them what leveraging is.

Schools and teachers don't teach you because they don't know what it is either. Your parents and your friends probably haven't taught you because they probably don't understand it either. Certainly your boss is not teaching you about leverage because she/he is leveraging YOU, and they don't want you to figure it out.

SO, What IS Leverage?

Leveraging has been around for thousands of years. Ancient man learned to use leverage to move heavy objects. Here is what probably happened:

Bork and Grog were two cavemen who had a problem. They had a really groovy bachelor cave set up for themselves. (It was the first man cave.) But, in the middle of the living room stood a huge boulder that they just couldn't move. It blocked the view of the great mud-pit games that were held every Sunday in the fall, so it was really important that they get rid of that boulder.

But, there was a problem. Bork and Grog were small cavemen. They didn't play in the mud games themselves and they spent most of their time sitting around on a soft tree trunk trying to invent things. (Sound familiar?) The bigger, stronger cavemen all made fun of them. It was sad.

However, one day, Grog got an idea. He brought a thick stick into the cave and placed a smaller rock next to the boulder. The two men used the stick as a *lever* and were able to move the rock. Actually, it was tough going at first. But, as they learned to use the lever more effectively (especially by moving the smaller rock closer to the boulder) they found it was easy to move that big boulder out of their man cave.

Unfortunately, it moved so well that it rolled down the hill and got stuck in the mud bowl game field, which stopped the game. In fact, it *disrupted* the game.

All the bigger cavemen struggled to move that boulder the old-fashioned way. They heaved, pulled, pushed and grunted. They spent a LOT of their time and effort trying to move that boulder, but they just couldn't do it.

Finally, Bork and Grog walked on to the field, in front of all those huge cavemen, and in front of all the cave people who were watching the game. Bork used the stick and Grog moved the smaller rock, and they moved the stone *almost all the way* out of the mud bowl field. And then they stopped…

History does not record exactly what happened next, but we think that Bork and Grog probably created a training video and made a fortune teaching other cavemen how to move boulders.

Leverage Gives You Power

Who were Bork and Grog? They were the ancestors of Joe and Mary Jo. They were just two ordinary cavemen who had a problem. They learned how a very simple tool could give ordinary people incredible power—the power to move huge obstacles.

Applying leverage means using your head, not your back. You start with something you own (in the case above, it was a stick and a small rock) and you apply it to your problem. Simple.

Now, how does this apply to business? And more particularly, how does it apply to YOUR business?

In the last two chapters, we talked about ownership and equity.

Ownership and equity are the keys to whether you are going to leverage or be leveraged.

If you own the tools, you can leverage. If you are just renting the tools from someone else, you are working for that person, and they are leveraging you.

First Things First, You Get Leveraged in Business

When you go to work, your boss pays you some money. How much does she pay you? She pays you just enough so that you will not quit! She wants to pay you the least amount she can and still have you do the work.

Why does she pay you such a small amount? Because you are just ONE tool in her powerful business. She is going to pay you some money and you are going to perform a job. Now, you are just ONE of the people doing that job. In fact, there may be thousands of people working at the same thing. Your boss coordinates your actions. You might not even know what your actions are doing in terms of the final, moneymaking sale of goods or services to the customers. In fact, at your job, you may never even SEE a customer during your entire career. It isn't necessary that you see the customer, because your job is simply your job.

Now, your boss has a plan. She (or he) looks out of her office window and sees the big picture. She is bringing in raw materials and getting that stuff into the hands of the people who do the manufacturing. Then, she coordinates the efforts of the sales force as they sell the finished stuff to customers. She also oversees the people who do all the administrative jobs like accounting and human resources.

Your boss, or her boss, or your boss's boss, or *somebody out there* actually OWNS the factory the raw material, the patents, etc. They are leveraging all the workers.

The company pays you and the other workers to do a small job and then they sell your work at a higher price to the customers. You see, if you are getting paid $20/hour by your boss, your work may actually be worth $50 per hour to the final customer. Now, if you are just one of hundreds of workers at your company, the company *leverages* your time many times over. They leverage your time, the guy next to you, the guy next to him, etc.

Companies, business people and especially business owners, *leverage* the time and talent of their employees to make money. The employees trade their time for dollars and the business owner makes a leveraged amount of money on that work.

So, Why Doesn't *Everyone* Leverage His or Her Time?

The answer to that question is quite simple: "Risk." There is a tremendous amount of risk involved in owning a business and that stops most people cold. Imagine building a factory and hiring all those people *before* you get even a single order. Or, what happens when another company comes along and cuts their prices and steals all your customers?

Folks, it is *risky* out there in the business world. It is tough. You are taking a chance when you build a business and leverage it. Yes, you can make a lot of money, but you can also lose your shirt!

UNLESS…

There is one way to get the advantage of leveraging without taking on the risk: find a company that really needs the one thing that you can bring them, and then let that company take the risk while you build a business.

Did you get that? Did you see the key phrase in that sentence? It is "The one thing that you can bring them…"

Folks, when you are in the right spot at the right time you can *leverage, leverage, leverage* if you are smart. If you listen to what companies, prospects and customers are saying—what they are asking for. If you learn to *listen* then you can *leverage*. And, you can make a whole boatload of money while you do it.

And here is the great news… you can reduce your risk to almost nothing!

But, Most People Aren't Listening…

Most of us, particularly in the United States, are trained from birth to be employees. We are not taught to *listen* to the right things. Yes, our parents, teachers and bosses keep telling us we have to listen, but they don't mean the "money-making" kind of listening. They mean the "do this exactly as I tell you to do it" kind of listening.

When your boss comes into your office and says, "We need these reports done by Tuesday afternoon so we can show them to the corporate chief," he ISN'T saying, "Here is an opportunity for you to take the resources of the corporation and make a pile of money for yourself." No, he is saying, "Don't make the same mistakes you made last time. Do exactly as I told you to do and don't ask questions."

How about your teachers or professors? Did they ever say, "Always look for opportunities to give a customer something special and then make a fortune by doing it again and again"?

Folks, you know that your boss, your parents, and your teachers love you. (Well, maybe not the boss.) They want the best for you. But let's face it. You aren't getting a lot of good leveraging advice out there, are you?

So now, here it comes. You are getting some great leveraging advice. We are showing you this for one reason—we want you to succeed at this business. We want you to finally, for once in your life, learn what Yoni is telling you. Don't listen to his words alone. Listen to your own business sense. And, if you don't have great business sense, then listen to people who do have it—people who are successful at the art of listening *and* leveraging for money.

So, How Do YOU Leverage?

You leverage by listening to what Jay and Yoni and Bill Hoffmann are telling you they NEED. They have this great business—low-cost warranties that will absolutely disrupt the way people buy warranties. (Remember, MILLIONS of people buy warranties every year and most of those warranties are over priced and sold at a moment of weakness to the customer.) They are saying, "We want to cause a huge disruption in this business and make a bundle of money. We know this industry is turned upside down. It just needs to be shaken and all the money will come tumbling out. We want to give people something they are not getting right now—fairly priced and highly effective warranties. But to do all that, we need YOU to do just one thing."

Folks, when you listen to what Yoni and Jay are saying, we want you to hear what we just wrote above. We don't want you to hear...

Blah, blah, blah, Warranty. Blah, blah, blah, Network Marketing.

That is what the leveraged classes are hearing! They don't know how to listen to what is really being said. You don't want to be part of the *leveraged* class. You want to be part of the *leveraging class* because that is where the money is. And, what you really want to do is become part of the *leveraging at no risk class.*

What My Warranty Rewards is Really Saying and What You Can do About it

Here is what My Warranty Rewards is really saying: "We know there is a huge market out there for fairly priced warranties. We know this because MILLIONS of people are buying *unfairly* priced warranties and MILLIONS more would buy warranties if they were fairly priced. But, we have a problem. We don't want to spend MILLIONS of dollars IN ADVANCE to reach these people. We already did all the things necessary to bring this warranty product to market. We have the product, the legal clearances, the experience, the offices, the accounting systems, etc. (Remember the last chapter: these are all the Equities that you need in business.)

But, we are missing just one thing. We need a group of people who are willing to tell others about this great product and opportunity. We are willing to train those people, and give them all the things they need to succeed. In other words, we will assume all of the risks. We will be the support, the system and the structure of the business. We aren't asking anyone to be our partners financially. We just need average people (aka Joe and Mary Jo) who are willing to tell other average people (all the Joes and Mary Jos you know) about this product and this opportunity.

We are going to put these average people in their own businesses. We will never stand in their way, nor discourage them. We NEED these great people in order to fulfill our mission. And, we are willing to share a HUGE percentage of the profits in order to get the confidence of these average people. We want them to believe in us. We will PAY for that belief. We will PAY for their effort.

But, we are not paying a wage. We are not paying a salary.

We are paying our business Agents with a piece of the action, and that piece can be as big as our Agents want it to be.

Folks that is what you should be hearing now. Imagine how powerful your leveraging activities can be now. You are putting almost NOTHING at risk (a couple of hundred dollars). Yet, you get unlimited opportunity. You get to use all the equities of My Warranty Rewards, INCLUDING the Mentor Equity of the leaders of that company.

They want just one thing from you—just tell some people about the product and the opportunity. That's it and that's great leverage.

Okay, NOW Do You Understand What Yoni Was Saying?

It is just a matter of listening. But, it also matters how you answer the call.

Chapter 13:
Break Even and Then *Break Out!*

"Poor people rent to own. Rich people own to rent."

—David Peters

Even when presented with a fabulous opportunity—an opportunity that will bring happiness, fortune and even Peace of Mind—most people can't get past the fear of making a mistake.

It isn't surprising really. In school, we lose points for the wrong answer. In our job, too many mistakes and we are fired. Even our family and friends may say, "Why did you try to do something different? People like us shouldn't get involved with that sort of thing."

And, for all these reasons, average Joes and Mary Jos stop looking at the opportunity to achieve something great and simply look at the small hurdle of fear. It stops them dead in their tracks. Instead of looking to successful people for inspiration, they look at successful people with suspicion. And then, ordinary men and women slip back into the fear and uncertainty that makes them accept the mediocrity of being average. Ironically, by worrying about a small risk, they expose themselves to a far greater risk.

The My Warranty Rewards Leadership Recognizes this Problem

When Jay Tuerk and Yoni Ashorav decided to take their low-cost warranties directly to the people who needed them, they made the decision to find the best Network Marketing Leaders in the business. And, when they found Bill Hoffmann, the three of them made a simple decision that would help the average Joe and Mary Jo overcome the fear that stops most ordinary people dead in their tracks.

Jay, Yoni and Bill created a company that would offer *immediate* rewards to every Independent Agent, and at the same time, would heavily reward any Agent who created a large network of other Agents. While this two-tier approach is not unique to My Warranty Rewards, it is rare to find a company that is so serious about it.

You see folks, at My Warranty Rewards the system is set up to allow anyone to get his/her money back. (Even though the amount of money that an Agent needs to start his/her business is quite small.) Jay, Yoni and Bill knew that it wasn't the *amount* of the money that mattered, it was the *feeling of insecurity* that made people feel uncomfortable.

By creating a two-tiered system of payouts (immediate bonuses for simple tasks and long-term payouts for bigger results) the trio of business people made it known that they understood what ordinary people go through. They understood why many people fail before they even get started.

Most People Never Achieve Success—at Any Level!

Here is a sad fact about modern American life. Most of us never really achieve success—even a small amount of it. Oh sure, we get jobs and make some money. Some of us may make money betting on stocks and bonds. (Oh, sorry, we meant to say, "investing in the market.") But few people EVER build something and profit from it.

Yes, our bosses may give us a bonus sometimes when we do something special at work, but how many average people see an opportunity, seize it, and actually make some money at it? It is almost unheard of, isn't it?

Think about it. How often have you done it? Have you kept your eyes open, seen something that others may not seem to see, built a business around it and then brought home some money to your family?

On the other hand, most of us have done something at work—something that either makes money for the company or saves it money—and received almost NO reward for it. We are not saying that everyone is crazy, we are just saying that most people never get the satisfaction of seeing their work rewarded with EXTRA MONEY! But, imagine how good it feels when you actually do get paid for your initiative. Think about how great it would be if you could say to your family, "Hey, let's take a vacation this week. I made some money doing _____."

Folks, we can tell you, it feels GREAT!

But, while this feels good, many people are afraid to try because they are afraid of *losing* money—no matter how little money it is.

It isn't a lack of high expectations that hold people back. It is a fear that they are going to be embarrassed.

The Secret to Breaking Even

Bill Quain likes the ponies. Do you know what that means? It means he likes going to the horse races. But Bill likes to win the Daily Double most of all. What is the Daily Double? It is a single ticket that you buy that picks the winner of the first race and the winner of the second race. Why does Bill like playing the Daily Double? Because, as he puts it, "If you win the Daily Double, the rest of the day you are *playing with the house's money!*" In other words, betting on the third race is a lot more fun if you are betting with the winnings from the Daily Double.

Jay, Yoni and Bill want you to play with the house's money. They want you to get some quick bonuses—right out of the gate (to continue the horse racing theme). They want you to get some immediate success so that you can look your friends in the eye and say, "I made money already!" They want you to be able to look at *yourself* with a feeling of accomplishment.

And so, they created a few fast bonuses that will give you your money back—and then some—for just a little work. If you follow their training you can be one of the people who have success almost immediately. After that, you are playing with the house's money. And, after getting some initial success, you can help *others* get that success. When you recruit some new Agents, you can look them in the eye and say, "Would you like to play with the house's money instead of your own?"

But in order to play with the house's money, you need to understand what "breaking even" is all about.

Breaking Even by Filling Up the Hole

When you become an Independent Agent for My Warranty Rewards, you make an investment of about $200. In addition, you are going to pay about $20 each month for your Business System, including your website, videos, training, etc.

In order to understand how to break even, think of the $200 as a hole in the ground. You need to fill up that hole with money. When you become an Agent, the hole is $200 deep. If you make $600 by working on the quick-start bonuses they have (see your website for details) you will *fill the $200-deep hole* and have $400 in profits—right away! Now, you are playing with the house's money. You are ahead. You have done what almost NONE of your friends have done. You have accomplished what almost NONE of your teachers ever did. You saw an opportunity and took it. You made a profit.

What can you do with the "house's money" after that? You can do whatever you want to do with it! You can use it to pay off the $20/month cost for your business platform or you could pay off some bills. Maybe you can take your family to a special day at an amusement park.

Folks, *whatever* you do with it, make sure you recognize that you are spending the house's money. This is money that you earned by doing something simple—but by doing something that most people never do.

Of course, we don't want you to stop there and YOU don't want to stop there. Once you get a taste for the house's money, we want you to get more than a taste. We want you to get a full meal—every day.

That is when you will look beyond break even, to break out actions.

Learning to Break Out

With My Warranty Rewards you have an opportunity to Break Out of "average" and into a world of achievement and success.

This is all part of the My Warranty Rewards Compensation Plan. We won't go into the particulars in this book, because you can get all the payout information on the website, but Breaking Out is one of life's great pleasures. It is something that you should experience—at least once in your life.

Look, we have already shown you that the Warranty Business is just right for *disruption*. In the coming months, millions of people are going to realize that their warranties are overpriced. They are going to learn about a new kind of warranty—low-cost, never-ending, and direct-to-consumers. This disruption happened in the music business (iTunes), the grocery business (Whole Foods) and in the Fast Food business (McDonalds) to name just a few industries.

What would have happened to your financial situation if you had been a part of this disruption? Would you have made lots and lots of money? Would you look like a hero right now if you had been smart enough and ambitious enough to get into those businesses—

with almost no risk? Of course you would look like a hero. You would certainly *feel like* a hero.

As a My Warranty Rewards Agent, you are poised to take advantage of a huge transfer of wealth. Money is going to shift from the Big Box Stores and into the hands of the Agents who build businesses of other Agents. Your income from My Warranty Rewards is going to depend on how many other Agents you can turn into business builders.

You will make money if you understand one thing – you are now in the business of building business builders.

The Business of Building Business Builders

If you ask the average *Network Marketing* Joe or Mary Jo "What business are you really in?" most of them would say, "I am in the _____ (soap, vitamin, power drink, energy, etc.) business." Technically, each of the average Joe and Mary Jos would be correct, but NONE of them would be getting wealthy from that answer. However, if one of them said, "I am in the business of building business builders," then THAT person would be the one you want in your downline.

Look, as great as the Warranty business is—a business that is on the verge of disruption—it is not the business you are in. You are NOT a Warranty millionaire-in-training. Warranties are only the *vehicle* you are driving to your success. Yes, it is a very attractive vehicle. You have no inventories or shipping costs. You are able to sell warranties *less expensively* than traditional retailers sell them. They are a product that MILLIONS of people want and when those millions of people begin to discover that they can get PERMANENT warranties at a low monthly fee, there is going to be a landslide of demand for YOUR product.

And while you can certainly make money by selling warranties, and in fact you WILL sell warranties to customers, your fortune, your long-term success, is dependent upon your ability to help other people do the same thing you are doing. In other words, you are in the business of building business builders. You are "looking for people who are looking." And when you find them, you need to help them grow their businesses, just like your upline is helping you grow yours.

Your Business Builder Bonus

What is the Business Builder Bonus that is built into the My Warranty Rewards Compensation Plan? It is simple. Your Business Builder Bonus is long-term, *dependable*, residual income. Here is the secret:

1. When you build Business Builders, you are building stability. The Business Builders in your downline have something to lose. They are making money and enjoying success. They aren't going to jeopardize that!

2. Your money is residual—it continues to come in, even when you are not working on your business. Why is that? Because you are getting paid for the efforts of others. When they are successful, you get paid. When they get paid, you get paid.

3. Your products are not a "one-and-done" sale. Your income is based on monthly payments from the people in your business. Each month they have a warranty, it becomes more valuable to them because those products are now one month older—and more likely to need replacement, repair or refunds. This is ongoing, stable income.

4. Most importantly, you are now *leveraging* your business. You took your small investment and reached break even quickly. You are now playing with the house's money. But you didn't stop there. You started helping other people break even and then started helping them become business builders. You are now getting paid for *their* success as well as your own. This is leverage. This is power, and this is success.

That is why we say, "Break Even and then Break Out." You are breaking out of the bonds that hold most ordinary men and women in virtual slavery to a job and a boss. You are breaking out of the class of people that are in debt with mortgages, credit cards, loans and other instruments of financial bondage.

"Breaking Out" Equals Freedom and Peace of Mind

You are in the Peace of Mind Business—Peace of Mind for you and for others. You are driving the right vehicle to your success. You have two stops along the journey. The first one is to Break Even. Don't waste a lot of time getting to this place. Remember, all you have to do is to fill in a $200-deep hole! The second stop isn't really a stop. It is a lifetime journey. You will find the road filled with really interesting people. These are other business builders. They are people with a dream. And, while their dreams may not be exactly the same as yours, the mere fact that you are all dream-building, business-building success stories will give you worthwhile friends for a lifetime.

We look forward to your "Breaking Out" journey, and to the friendships we will all form together.

Chapter 14:
You Have the Last Word

A Special Note from Jay Tuerk, Yoni Ashurov, Bill Hoffmann, and Bill Quain

What a pleasure this has been—sharing the *Why*, the *What* and the *How* of your success with you. By now, you have learned a lot about the Peace of Mind Business, The Warranty Business, and the Business of Building Business Builders. And we could end this book with more words from us—summarizing all that we have said. But this isn't about us. It isn't even about Peace of Mind, Warranties, Leveraging and Growing a Business.

This book is written for you. It is all about YOU and what you want and need in life. It is written with one thing in mind—to help you get what you want.

So, we thought it might be fun to let you have the last word. And we thought it might be even more fun if you could read the words and thoughts of people just like you. We are all in this great journey together: your thoughts and the thoughts of other Agents are what will drive this business.

To help you with this, we set up a website and blog at *www.MWRblog.com*.

When you go there, you will find an up-to-date journal and forum for My Warranty Rewards Agents. We invite you to share your thoughts, your dreams, and your success stories.

And while you are there, how about sharing your answers to the following questions:

1. What did you learn about Peace of Mind from this book? How will this help you make a difference in your life? What is your biggest Peace of Mind Goal?

2. What did you learn about the Warranty business from this book? Why is this the best business for business builders right now? What is your favorite "warranty story" from your personal experience?

3. Why are you in this business? What do you think about personal business ownership? Do you like the idea of being a business builder and building a business of business builders?

Folks, we want to keep you engaged in this business—in real time. We look forward to building a relationship with you and helping you build your personal fortune as you achieve Peace of Mind.

Welcome to the Team—the Peace of Mind Team.

Appendix A

Sample Disrupter List with Categories

Take a look at the list of comments below and notice the categories we assigned to each comment.

Categories:
1 – Financial (with two subsets – "employment" and "property")
2 – Health
3 – Family/Relationships
4 – Legal/Technological
5 – Self-Worth/Self-Image

Disrupter Comment List with Categories

Assigned Category	Comment
1	After working all day, I am too tired to shop for food or cook.
1	All this technology is expensive.
4	Can't anyone teach me how to use my iPad?
1	Do I have enough money to retire?
4	Every time I buy something for my kids, it breaks.
1	Everyone is shopping for food at the same time as I am, and the lines take forever. But, I have to wait until I have time off from work to shop.
1	He hasn't made the child support payments in over three months.
1	How am I going to pay for my kids' college education?
3	How am I going to tell my father he can't drive anymore?
1	How will I pay for long-term care for myself or for my parents?
5	I am lonely all the time.
1	I am worried that I don't have enough insurance.

1	I am worried that I have too much insurance.
1	I am worried that there will be another recession.
1	I bought some stock and it is not doing well.
3	I can never get my child to call me back to let me know she is okay.
1	I can't afford the medicine I need to be healthy.
1	I can't afford to pay for all the data my family uses on their cell phones.
1	I can't afford to pay my property taxes. They keep going up.
4	I can't seem to keep track of all the paperwork in my life.
4	I can't seem to learn how to use this new technology.
1	I can't seem to pay off my credit card bills.
5	I don't even know how to get started on making changes.
4	I don't even know if I have warranties on some of my stuff.
1	I don't feel like I am in the right job, but it is the only one I can get right now.
1	I don't have the money to buy healthy foods for my family.
3	I don't seem to have any close friends anymore.
1	I had to take a pay cut to keep my job.
1	I have a variable rate mortgage and I am worried about my payments going up.
1	I just got a call that my kid is sick and I have to pick her up, but I have a big meeting I can't miss.
3	I just got served with divorce papers.
2	I just got some bad news at the doctor's office.
1	I keep getting sick and missing work.
2	I keep hearing about the side effects of medicines I take. It worries me.
1	I kept putting off those reports and now they are late.
3	I miss my husband/wife since he/she passed away.

1	I miss the good old days when you got what you paid for. Everything cost less.
3	I missed my kid's recital because I had to work.
5	I never get credit for my good ideas.
3	I never know what my spouse is thinking.
1	I owe more on my house than it is worth.
1	I want to take a cruise with my spouse to celebrate our anniversary, but I haven't got the time or money to do it.
3	I worry about my kid getting bullied online.
3	I worry about my kid not being popular.
3	I worry about my kids at day care.
3	I worry about my kids coming home to an empty house.
1	If my old car breaks down, I can't get to work.
1	Is my car going to die soon?
3	Is my husband cheating on me?
1	Is there going to be another bad winter this year? I can't afford the heating bill.
5	It would be nice to be appreciated for a change.
4	Life is just too complicated these days.
1	My boss came up with some crazy ideas at work. I will have to work harder.
4	My child is in trouble and I have to hire a lawyer – I can't afford it.
4	My computer's hard drive crashed yesterday. All my documents and photos were on there.
1	My credit cards have very high interest.
3	My diabetic daughter will not check her blood sugar levels.
3	My ex-husband's lawyer is driving me crazy.
1	My house is falling apart, but I can't afford to get it repaired.
4	My internet keeps turning on and off.

1	My kid had an accident and the insurance payments are through the roof.
2	My kid has food allergies and I worry about them all the time.
3	My kid just learned to drive. I am worried about him/her having an accident.
3	My kids are growing up so quickly and I never have time to spend with them.
3	My marriage is falling apart.
1	My parents are getting older and need financial help from me.
3	My parents are getting older and their health is failing.
4	My phone broke and I lost all my contacts.
1	My sales quota is so high that I can't possibly reach it.
3	My son/daughter is engaged to marry someone we just can't stand.
1	My wife wanted to stay home after the baby was born, but we couldn't afford it.
3	My wife/husband is depressed all the time.
5	Nobody seems to care about me.
3	One of the people I work with keeps telling stories about me to others.
1	Our neighborhood is terrible. I am afraid to come home at night.
5	People like me will never have money.
5	People like me will never succeed, so why try?
1	The bus drivers' union is about to go on strike. How will I get to work?
1	The long commute is killing me.
3	The romance has gone out of our marriage. We are just so busy and so stressed out about things.
1	The traffic on my commute is driving me crazy.
1	There have been a lot of layoffs at work. I am worried about losing my job.

1	There is never enough money to pay the bills each month.
5	They don't appreciate me at work.
4	Things were better when life was simpler.
1	The IRS is auditing us.
1	We are falling behind in some of our payments. They might take the car.
1	We have to shop at Sam's Club, and the boxes and bags are too big to store.
3	We haven't had a family vacation in years.
1	What if I can't afford the best school that my kid wants to attend?
1	What if I can't afford to buy a safe car for my kid?
3	What if I don't have the time or money to go visit my aging parents?
2	What if I get every disease I see on television?
2	What if I get sick and can't work?
1	What if my kid wants to get married and I can't afford the wedding?
3	What if my kids never leave the house?
5	What if someone younger replaces me at work?
1	What if the stock market crashes and I lose all my investments?
1	When are they going to stop construction on these roads? I am always late for work and appointments.
4	When something breaks, I can never find the warranty papers.